THE ELEVEN YOGIC ARTS OF CREATIVE LIVING

THE ELEVEN YOGIC ARTS OF CREATIVE LIVING

LOOKING AT THE TEACHINGS OF YOGI BHAJAN THROUGH THE LENS OF CREATIVITY

RAGHUBIR KHALSA KINTISCH

STRIPED DOG PRESS

"THE WHOLE CONCEPT OF SPIRITUALITY IS A GIFT FROM THE ARTISTS OF THE WORLD TO THE WORLD.  IF WRITERS HAD NOT WRITTEN, THERE WOULD BE NO SCRIPTURES. IF SCULPTORS HAD NOT SCULPTED, THERE WOULD BE NO GODS FOUND IN THE TEMPLES. IF PAINTERS HAD NOT PAINTED THERE WOULD HAVE BEEN NO VISUALS TO MEDITATE ON. THE REALITY IS THAT REAL SAINTS WERE REAL ARTISTS. FROM THEIR AWARENESS THEY CONTEMPLATED, CONCENTRATED, MEDITATED, AND CAME OUT WITH THE SYMBOLS WHICH WERE IMMEDIATELY ACCEPTED AND ADOPTED. ACCORDING TO THE VEDAS, ALL PEOPLE WERE IN THE BEGINNING ARTISTS. THROUGH THOSE VISIONARY ARTISTS WHO DEVOTED THEMSELVES COMPLETELY TO SPIRITUAL LIFE ALL THE SYMBOLS OF ART CAME OUT. THAT IS WHY ART AND SPIRITUALITY ARE INSEPARABLE."
HARISH JOHARI

TABLE OF CONTENTS

ACKNOWLEDGING YOUR LINEAGE

In any discipline, spiritual, artistic or otherwise, we always invoke the presence and gratitude for the Masters; the teachers who came before us. This is a time-honored tradition that has its place, necessity and value in any situation where one person learns from another.

You could look back on your life and I am sure there are some people; an aunt or uncle, a parent, a few school teachers, a friend, a friend's parent, a salesperson at a local store, etc. who have left you with a pearl or two of wisdom. If you have studied any of the arts, I am positive there are teachers and mentors in your past who lit you up from within. I know there were a few of those in mine. And if you are lucky in this life to meet your spiritual teacher, not only would you give thanks to the immeasurable lessons and blessings that you received from your teacher, but to the lineage from which they came.

Acknowledging your lineage is a practice that is as old as the hills. It nurtures humility and grants protection and guidance. It is a form of gratitude, the blessings of which are immeasurable. I always tell art students that before they begin work on a project that they should take a moment to give thanks to the teachers and artists who inspired them. Artisans always "belonged" to the studio of their masters having most likely started out as apprentices there; it was an honor to claim the tradition in which you were trained. Dancers, Actors, and Artists enthusiastically tip their hats to their mentors, teachers or the school at which they were trained; it often acts as a dossier, letting people know the quality and sincerity of their work. In the martial arts, the name of the schools are as numerous as the senseis who started them. In fact in all spiritual traditions, an invocation to the masters in one's lineage, is essential before beginning one's practice.

In Kundalini Yoga we chant Ong Namo Guru Dev Namo before we begin our yoga practice because in doing so, we honor and connect to those who came before us; the masters and teachers who we refer to as "the Golden Chain." It is a requirement that we chant it a minimum of three times before we practice. The Golden Chain consists of your teacher, your teacher's teacher, your teacher's teacher's teacher and so on.In my case, I invoke gratitude for my teacher, Harijiwan and his teacher Yogi Bhajan and his teacher Sant Hazara Singh all the way back through the House of Guru Ram Das. This sign of respect is fundamental no matter what you do or what you create; expressing gratitude is a fundamental ingredient of any spiritual or creative practice.

Ong Namo Guru Dev Namo is a good place to start for this book as well.

The common translation is "I bow to the teacher within". Ong is the sound of creativity. When pronounced correctly, Yogi Bhajan said that the entire electro-magnetic field of the Universe becomes yours.

"Dev" means transparent. "Guru" means who brings light into darkness. I bow to you "Ong Namo". Oh creative total self. " - Yogi Bhajan, 1990

IN GRATITUDE

I have always felt the touch of guidance and support of the Universe so I deeply appreciate the ease with which my life has unfolded thus far.

I am deeply, deeply grateful to my teacher Harijiwan who has over the years generously given me so many blessings and opportunities; that I might acknowledge and use my strengths for the greater good, to become a better teacher of Kundalini Yoga and to always bring truth and grace to everything I do.

I'd like to acknowledge the Yogi Bhajan Library of Teachings; an expansive ocean of tapes, recordings, transcripts, historical notes, exercises and meditations that is free and completely accessible. If you read a quote from Yogi Bhajan in this volume, chances are that it came from this priceless archive. Donating to this wonderful online resource is highly recommended to keep it free for all.

I appreciate all the teachers and students in this Kundalini Yoga practice who have always held the bar high for me and for each other. Building community and being of service in that community is meditation in action and a beautiful practice; the sangat is a true blessing.

I am grateful for all the opportunities in this life to be of service. Seva is an honor and a privilege; if you ever have the opportunity to serve, do it. It is a life changer.

I feel tremendous gratitude to have been blessed by so many Great Ones in this life. The generosity I have received in all its myriad forms have been plentiful and I hope that I have done well by those who shared their energy and wisdom with me. My goal is that I may be able to do the same for others.

At sixty, I went back to academia to get my MFA in Public Practice at OTIS College of Art and Design. Dedicating two years to my artistic and academic growth required a lot of sacrifice and hard work. So I am grateful to my patron, my cohort and all my incredible professors, mentors, advisors, and fellow students that I studied with. They kept it very real and inspired me to keep up. I am inspired and amazed by each and every one of my art students so a big shout out goes to them, too. They keep my mind flexible and my communication skills sharp, but most of all, I learn as much (if not more) from them, than what they learn from me.

I don't get to write a gratitude page very often and while I'm on the subject, it wouldn't be complete unless I thanked all the art and music teachers in my life who pushed my buttons throughout the years. As a teaching artist, I hope that I will have as profound and lasting an effect on the young artists I teach now, as the teachers who have taught me. Grateful beyond measure to them all…even to the ones whose names I can't remember. But here's to the ones I do:

Thank you Mr. Hobart, Roberta Berlin, Alan Levine from the junior high school and high school years; Bob Hamilton, Gerry Immonen, and Dean Richardson from the RISD years; Dave Caballero and Bobby Matos for accordion and Afro-Cuban percussion lessons, respectively; and the magnificent creative avatars from the OTIS Public Practice Program - Dana Duff, Renee Petropoulos, Suzanne Lacy, Chelo Montoya, Anuradha Vikram, Karen Moss, Andrea Bowers, Sandra de la Loza, Mario Ybarra, Jr., and Annetta Kapon. Each and every one of these masterful, inspirational mentors held me accountable for my creative commitments.

A big thank you to Zoë for making it so easy, creative and fun to be a mom. This is not the first time we've been together; I am certain we've been switching roles back and forth for a long, long time. I am so grateful to Jacob who loves her with all his heart.

Thank you to all the gurus in my life… all my exceptional friends and family that have always seen me as I am and have loved me dearly in spite of it. Unconditional Love is a rare fruit and I have enjoyed its sweetness my entire life. …you all know who you are:

Shout-out to the nuclear fam: The 143 crew, N & P, SS, Sherlock & RP, LM, LH & RH, LR, LY, PR, KR, MS & WS, BM & MVH, DJ Kaputnik, MS & BS, LM, ET, NK, SSK, NS, LL, TKK, LLS & MD, AC, LL & MC, CC & AC, JF, SGS, JGK, ND & CE, JH, NS, KK, ARK & BK, EE & MG, SB, M&M and so, so, so many others…

I have profound gratitude for my very first set of cray-pas and the instructions I received with them: *"If you want to make a masterpiece you must cover the entire page".* The same person also gave me this sage advice: *"You don't have to go looking for God in a temple or church…God resides right here in your heart ".*

I have so much appreciation for the teachings of Yogi Bhajan; for this radical technology that changed my life. From the very first time I bowed my head after I taught my very first class until today, I give silent thanks: Thank you for bringing these teachings to me and allowing me to share them with others. Sat Nam.

WHO IS YOGI BHAJAN?

I practice and teach Kundalini Yoga as taught by Yogi Bhajan. For those not familiar with Yogi Bhajan or his teachings, he arrived in Los Angeles virtually unknown in 1968 and shared the secret teachings of Kundalini Yoga with young spiritual seekers of the era. He immediately recognized that the experience of higher consciousness they were attempting to find through drugs, could be achieved by practicing the Science of Kundalini Yoga, while simultaneously rebuilding their nervous systems. Breaking the centuries old tradition of secrecy surrounding the empowering science of Kundalini Yoga, he began teaching it publicly.

With yogic technology of meditation, physical exercises and postures, yogic philosophy, and loving acceptance, he gave an effective alternative to a self-destructive and non-productive way of life which was making people feel stuck and uninspired.

Inspired and motivated by Yogi Bhajan's words and adhering to the practices he taught, his students got creative! Tons of music, art, poetry and creative businesses flowed forth; reflecting the connection to the Universal flow of consciousness he shared with everyone. In addition to writing and speaking extensively about Creativity, Yogi Bhajan's expertise and influence affected people in all fields and from all walks of life; in the healing arts, the business world, in the arts, religion, government and sports. You could say that he embodied a rare combination of spiritual and down-to-earth practical wisdom which anyone can apply to any aspect of life.

His teachings inspire me because they are both practical and mystical and are organized in such a way as to be accessible to all.

- *Transformation is the driving force behind all creative endeavors*

- *Everyone is creative and everything we do is an expression of the Creative Flow*

- *I teach therefore I am. I have found teaching to be the greatest act of service and one of the highest creative arts*

- *And why do I teach? Teaching teaches me how to become a better student*

- *Creativity is flexibility of mind, body and spirit*

- *If, as Yogi Bhajan said, the purpose of creativity is to create an impact, what kind of impact do YOU want to make on this world?*

Raghubir

INTRODUCTION

"Creativity is not just for artists. It's for businesspeople looking for a new way to close a sale; it's for engineers trying to solve a problem; it's for parents who want their children to see the world in more than one way." - Twyla Tharp, dancer and choreographer

I have been an "artist" my whole life. From the time I could hold a piece of chalk in my hand, I knew that was what I was. I was also a spiritual seeker and craved mysticism and ritual in my life for as long as I can remember. I questioned the existence and meaning of God from the moment I first heard "that word". I grew up in a Jewish home where neither ritual nor mysticism played a big part.

My father was an track coach and so his parenting strategy utilized sports metaphors with a big emphasis on discipline and self-confidence. My mother was a musician and so her strategy leaned heavily on musical references with a big emphasis on practice and self-expression. I was encouraged at an early age to be exactly who I was and that's pretty much the approach I took my whole life. As creatively supportive a beginning as that all was, I still yearned for the cosmic connection to something I knew existed beyond the little finite me; something else, something more.

I studied many Eastern traditions on my own that I read about in books. I burned incense, dabbled in mysticism, embroidered jeans jackets with psychedelic designs, attended lectures in hippie bookstores, rode around with my friends in VW microbuses, painted weird surrealist  canvases, wore Indian clothing, played the guitar, studied yoga and meditation and did what every other young hippie did in the early 1970's except I did not discover Yogi Bhajan and Kundalini Yoga until much, much later.

When I happened upon Kundalini Yoga, I was already a grown up and had a successful career as an artist and designer. My daughter was in high school and I was beginning to teach art there. Everything looked pretty good from the outside, but inside of me, it wasn't. I wasn't in either the greatest state of mind or health and I was looking to recommit myself to a yoga and meditation practice which I had all but given up. The first "official" Kundalini Yoga class I took was an Iyengar class on the schedule - the style of yoga I had been previously practicing - but when I heard the mantra "Wahe Guru", I knew my life was never going to be the same.

As an artist, I had established a regular discipline and had experienced great transcendent moments during the practice of my art. These moments were somewhat predictable in that when I applied myself to my art on a regular basis and for a specific amount of time, those moments were almost guaranteed. Even though I experienced some blissful moments inside of my pre-Kundalini yoga days, it was nothing like I had experienced inside of that first "accidental" Kundalini Yoga class.

When I started practicing Kundalini Yoga regularly, the most remarkable thing I noticed was similarity in how I felt to when I was making art. I had never felt that way before, except when I was experiencing deep pure love for example, after the birth of my daughter. Because Kundalini energy, plain and simple, is your potential creative energy, the effects you feel either doing yoga or making art are very much the same. And when your inside matches your outside, it means you are in balance and there is no way you that cannot feel content and fulfilled.

The benefits of the Kundalini Yoga far exceed the confines of the art studio or yoga studio; I noticed that every action I took in my life was infused with a new level of consciousness and purpose.

Often people who start practicing Kundalini Yoga experience some form of new-found clarity and that is why it is called the "yoga of awareness". Of course this new awareness precipitates transformation and so I noticed that things that were stuck for a long time were finally moving and improving. I made better choices in all my endeavors and, as a result it came back to me tenfold. This return on my investment was so powerful that is was hard not to notice. It was hard for other people not to notice. I had more energy, somehow it created more time and my creative output exploded.

The teachings of Kundalini Yoga as taught by Yogi Bhajan® are filled with references to Creativity and accessing the Creative Flow. I decided to write this book because the subject of creativity is what Iam most passionate about and I have first-hand experience of what a dedicated spiritual practice can do for your creativity and what a dedicated artistic practice can do for your spirituality.

Creativity is not just what happens in a studio and it is not just reserved for people who make art. Creativity is for everyone; every single one of us is a creative being. The sooner we all start acting on this reality, the sooner our lives will improve and blossom.

I am an artist and an arts educator and so I spend a lot of time investigating and thinking about Creativity; what is it? Where does it come from? How do we get it? How can we manage it? What do we have to do to keep it going?

"For me, artistic activity is a spiritual activity that all artists practice." - Robert Filliou

I've listened to hundreds of Yogi Bhajan lectures, read countless transcripts and have written about his teachings in my blogs and newsletters. I discovered that what artists, musicians, writers, performers, actors, dancers, and athletes had to say about living creatively was similar, if not identical to what Yogi Bhajan was saying.

 I've devoured books, articles and videos in order to learn what makes other creative minds tick; what they had to say about being "in the flow", making an impact, tapping into the universal mind, how to nurture and grow ideas, humility in the face of inspiration, how to take care of one's "instrument", building a community of like minds, and of course, the magic of discipline and practice. In all cases, creatives were having spiritual experiences through the pursuit of their art, and those in pursuit of some sort of spiritual awakening found either a birth or rebirth of their creative selves.

The Eleven Yogic Arts of Creative Living is about re-framing how you think about creativity and how your life can transform as a result. You can practice it in any field or life situation in which you are desiring to be more courageous, self-expressed, happy and fulfilled. The most beautiful thing about the technology of Kundalini Yoga is that you can apply it to the life you are living right now - you don't have to stop doing what you are already doing. All it will do is make what ever you are doing, better. And that's the truth.

Peace, Love and Sat Nam,

Raghubir,

Los Angeles, 2020

ART OF THE UNIVERSAL MIND

"For the awakened individual, however, life begins now, at any and every moment; it begins at the moment when he realizes that he is part of a great whole, and in the realization becomes himself whole. In the knowledge of limits and relationships he discovers the eternal self, thenceforth to move with obedience and discipline in full freedom." - Henry Miller, writer and artist

We simply cannot talk about yoga and creativity without discussing the Universal Mind. Many have considered it to be the binding force of all life; that our own individual consciousness is just a part of the one universal consciousness much like a drop of water is part of the ocean. The Universal Mind is agreed on by scientists, artists, and spiritual practitioners to be a vast sea of vibrating energy that permeates through all that exists - an entire spectrum of mental existence and live potential in the Universe. This concept has been captivating both artists and truth seekers since the beginning of time; *chitta*, Buddha nature, Christ Consciousness and The Absolute are just a few of the other names it goes by.

If we are all made of energy and everything around us is made of energy and we are connected with everything through energy, then we and the universal mind or God or whatever you want to call it are one and the same. It is the source of everything; what we say or how we act is vibrated into this energy field and therefore everyone and everything is connected and affected in some way either directly or indirectly.

One of my favorite teachings from Yogi Bhajan on the Universal Mind is: *"wherever you will plug your mind, that you shall be".*

That sounds pretty simple and straight forward, doesn't it? When you plug your mind into feeling sorry for yourself, guess who's throwing a pity party? How many times have you felt stuck and like there was no way out; as though all your options had disappeared? You invest your mind in a juicy no-way-out scenario and bingo you're surrounded by a fortress of your own making. Or maybe you started worshipping the goddess of struggle who endows you with the power of thinking that no matter what you did, things didn't get any better? You are not alone! SO many of us get stuck in a loop of self-pity or self-sabotage yet it doesn't have to be that way.

Artists get stuck in similar loops of insecurity about their work or periods where nothing seems to come out right. The *Artist's Block* is very much "a thing"; a kind of romantic, feel-sorry-for-yourself period of inertia. In any case, these periods of emotional turmoil and non-movement can be eradicated by plugging into the Universal Mind. Instantly, emotion and commotion become devotion. Woes become possibilities. It's magical, really.

"You are a link of this entire creation. You are here for a purpose. No element can be formed without a missing molecule, is it not a scientific law? And are we not a unit mind molecule of that whole universal mind? And how can this planet be beautiful without you? But you create heat. You create friction, and that is where you make the planet ugly. Otherwise there is no reason to even think. You are a part of the universal mind and when you plug yourself in, you become universal mind and the beauty is all desires of the universal mind are pre-fulfilled and all desires of a limited mind have to be fulfilled. And there are many examples where it can be proved. A limited mind ends up all life hassling, a universal mind does not hassle at all". - Yogi Bhajan

The Kundalini Energy is your creative potential and is the link between your infinite and finite selves. Most of the time through these Kundalini yogic practices or in a particularly resonant creative flow moment, you can actually experience the existence of this Universal Cosmic Consciousness, God, Universal Mind, Fearlessness, Great Compassion, Grace, Truth, Purity, Love…or whatever you want to call it. You receive everything from it and can merge with it.

When spiritual practitioners come together to meditate, they create a forcefield that is made up of many individual minds, a collaborative magnetic field if you will, that if directed properly, can be tuned into the Universal Mind to affect tremendous change.

If you tune yourself to the vibratory frequency of the Universal Mind, everything will come to you.

CREATIVE POTENTIAL VS. THE EGO

"To be cured, we must rise from our graves and throw off the cerements of the dead. Nobody can do it for another - it is a private affair which is best done collectively. We must die as egos and be born again in the swarm, not separated and self-hypnotized, but individual and related." - Henry Miller

A creative person can reach a significant magnetic frequency through the practice of their art or craft and the pump thus primed, can initiate a flood of thought waves, feelings, impulses, and fearlessness (often referred to as "being in the flow" or "being in the zone") in which one is caught in the blissful flow of creative energy. What is truly remarkable is that both the artist and the spiritual practitioner achieve, whether consciously or unconsciously, certain points of concentration and breath patterns which alter the brain chemistry and glandular system, thus creating the same open-hearted feeling of contentment and oneness. Yogi Bhajan referred to the kundalini energy as "our creative potential". Once awakened, the kundalini energy will move through the mind, body and spirit connecting us to the Universal Mind and thus initiating the Creative Flow. There's a science to awakening it but it takes discipline to keep it moving.

The Universal Mind's only enemy is the ego. In Kundalini Yoga, we say that when we relate to the Universal Mind we relate to the highest and most divine part of ourselves, the soul. Intuitive, creative, and powerful, the Soul is who we "really" are. The ego stands in the way of being our most authentic self and in almost everything we teach and practice in Kundalini yoga, the eradication of the ego is at its core. I tend to think of the relationship between the Universal Mind and the Ego as being like the Superman/Clark Kent paradox; where the Universal Mind is, the ego is not.

"Therefore man has to understand one thing. Man is always limited and he even becomes limited when he has some sort of ego, he becomes unlimited when he becomes ego less, because until you do not give yourself to the unlimited you cannot become unlimited. This is a simple tuning of the mind. Plug your mind into the unlimited Ek Ong Kar, the one unlimited Creator whose energy flow in this universe, you shall become unlimited and so long you go on attaching or plugging your mind into the limited self you shall be limited. It is a simple basic law on which you must walk. Whatever you want your destination is your problem because you are the one who are to seek the God consciousness, you want to seek it in a limited manner it is fine, cool with me. If you want to seek it in unlimited manner, it is perfect. But must you remember wherever you will plug your mind, that you shall be."

Everyone is creative; the ability is inherent in all beings because Creativity is the natural law. Yogi Bhajan said that the creative flow was the purpose of life; that we create the flows, good or bad, that bring meaning and direction to our lives. Perfect and in the flow when we are born, some of us lose touch with our creative selves as we age; forgetting that each and every day is an opportunity for creating the life we want; creating the trends and the flows. We forget that when we take control of our identity, we are clearing the path for the creative cosmic energy to pass from the Universal Mind through us and to the world. Some artists even forget that their gifts and their creative ideas come from beyond them and end up taking all the credit for themselves. This lack of humility and gratitude is fed by the ego; the nemesis of the Universal Mind.

Of course there are many artists that acknowledge and respect the unlimited source of creativity that is a characteristic of the Universal Mind. They also understand that it is an energetic well from which and through which all sound, light and vibrations emanate.

"I believe that all people are in possession of what might be called a Universal Musical Mind. Any true music speaks with this Universal Mind to the Universal Mind in all people. The understanding that results will vary only in so far as people have or have not been conditioned to the various styles of music in which the universal mind speaks. Consequently, often some effort and exposure is necessary in order to understand some of the music coming from a different period or a different culture than that to which the listener has been conditioned." - Bill Evans, pianist and educator

The ego is responsible for cutting off the creative flow and your relationship with the Universal Mind. Controlling your mind is not only a way to achieve the balance necessary to connect to the Universal Mind, but the key to using your creative potential as well. Your mind's job is to serve your soul, but most of us use it for creating emotional intrigue, instead. Remember it's not your soul that gets angry, feels resentful, harbors hostility, and has no humility... it is your ego. When you take control of your mind and your emotions, you can quiet the ego and put it in its place. Your liberation in this life body is possible only through practical humility. When you feel that you have been created by your creator to serve humanity through your creativity, then you are serving, not manipulating. Serving is a major part of Creative Living.

The bottom line is, if you want to be healthy and happy, you must learn to control your mind. Wherever you direct, focus, plug your mind, that is where you will be. Put your mind in the Universal Mind, and your life will unfold in the most beautiful fashion, without limits and boundaries. Your limitlessness will inspire and uplift others, breed compassion, love and creativity, and ultimately transform the planet.

HOW CAN I PLUG INTO THIS UNIVERSAL MIND?

Cultivating promoting habits like feeling and expressing gratitude, practicing generosity, engendering humility, and being of service are some of the practices that will give engender a tangible relationship with the Universal Mind. According to the Yoga Sutras of Patanjali (the ancient authoritative text on yoga) the word "yoga" means union; in other words to yoke or join together. When you join the finite self with the infinite self through Kundalini yoga and meditation, you can experience many profound mystical feelings such as a merging of one's little self into a sea of consciousness, expansive compassion and understanding, improved health and vitality, reduced stress and worry, increased prosperity, more love, magical coincidences and last, but not least, continuous ever-flowing creative energy.

If in your conscious mind you can navigate the terrain of the subconscious mind to get to the Universal Mind and also to reconfigure your vibratory frequency so that it affects the electro-magnetic field around you, you will create enough magnetism to attract all the things you need and repel the things you don't. This gives you a healthy, creative, happy, and productive existence where you are sovereign and mighty.

As a creative person, you can reconfigure your vibratory frequency to pick up signals that are beneficial to your creative process, ideas and would-be ideas still functioning as wave-forms, opportunities and collaborators; in other words all that you need to bring a project to fruition.

The two most effective Universal Mind plug-ins are using breath and using mantra. Long deep breathing aka conscious breathing will calm you and bring you the feeling of oneness that is a characteristic of the Universal Mind. It is the cornerstone of the Kundalini Yoga practice (as well as all yoga practices) because it activates the parasympathetic nervous system, helps to remove toxins, cleans the blood, increases alertness, increases the flow of prana, in addition to aligning you with the Universal Energy Field. The greatest plus is that you can do it anywhere, anytime, and in any situation where you need grounding, to center yourself, or connect to your higher consciousness. Breathing shallowly causes anxiety, depression and panic because it doesn't stimulate the glandular system to secrete the hormones your brain needs to be happy and it will ultimately negatively affect your health and your immune system, too. There so many effective yogic breath patterns to use to connect you with Universal Mind; my personal favorite is the One Minute Breath; inhale for 20 seconds, hold for 20 seconds, and exhale for 20 seconds. More on this later...

Positive statements and affirmations are great and they can create big changes but chanting or listening to mantra is much more effective tool for awakening the soul. Mantra is the creative projection of the mind through sound; a formula that alters the patterns of the brain and can even change the vibrational frequency of a space. There's a technology called Shabad Guru which essentially translates into "the sound that is the teacher that transforms you." The Shabad (or sound) is not just any sound..it has the elements necessary to cut away your ego.

Japa is the practice of repeating mantra; it is a conscious recitation that changes the frequency of all of our words. You don't have to believe in anything to chant or listen to them. Anyone can use them. The mantras work because of the science of Naad, a balanced universal pattern of sounds. When you are chanting, your tongue moves over the 84 reflex points in the roof of the mouth which in turn vibrate the 72,000 energy channels in the body. Yogi Bhajan said, *"As you vibrate, the Universe vibrates with you."*

The tongue stimulates the meridian points in the upper palate in the same way your fingers type at a computer keyboard, only the computer is located in the hypothalamus in the brain. The hypothalamus communicates with the pituitary and pineal glands which regulate the endocrine system and its hormone secretions. This is what changes your blood chemistry, releases stored subconscious patterns of thinking and feeling, conquers depression, increases intuition, improves intelligence, relieves pain and connects you to the Infinite Creative flow. If you are looking for a way to program your consciousness to be in alignment with your soul, there is nothing as effective and powerful as the technology of mantra.

UNIVERSAL MIND AND COMPASSIONATE ACTIVISM

The directed attunement of many minds is referred to as Global Consciousness and when it is used as a viable non-violent method for social and political change, it is called Subtle, Spiritual, or

Compassionate Activism. When we become aware, we end up activating our lives. When groups become aware, it becomes a social, spiritual, creative and political activation. This kind of activation is only possible with the existence and power of the Universal Mind force.

All the world's major spiritual and/or religious traditions have used the Universal Mind's collective energy for group as well as for individual benefit. For example, practitioners of one of the world's most ancient religious traditions, shamans - who were often consulted on individual healing and problem solving - were essentially the ecological and spiritual guardians of the tribe as a whole. Through shamanic guidance, a community could activate transformation for the benefit of all through group trance, prayer and ritual. According to Vedic tradition, mantras and sounds have the ability to change reality (or the energetic structure of one's experience of time and space) so that the combined effect of a group meditation could be absolutely revolutionary.

"It is the same mind which vibrates in everyone. So if you can make your mind strong then you have not to hassle, then the universal mind will serve you. But if your mind is not strong you have to hassle. You know swimming through an ocean twenty miles and going in a boat can give you a direct experience. When universal mind serves you, everything is cool, calm, quiet, peaceful. When it doesn't, you won't. Swimming is good in a swimming pool and it is good in weekend when you go for a retreat in an ocean. But man, if you are brought right in the middle of the ocean, it's very difficult. When you do not know who you are, where you are, why you are, when you will see the shore, when you will get your food, what is going to happen. It's terrible. So try to locate your longitude

and latitude and see where you are and from there, start it. Everything will workout for the better."

In addition to using the powerful current of the Universal Mind to shift cultural behavior, it is a living, pulsating archive of electro-magnetic waves, vibrations and signals not unlike the airwaves from which we glean satellite, radio or television broadcasts. When talking about creativity and yoga, it must be understood that the Universal Mind is a huge unlimited well of creative ideas just waiting to be downloaded. Just like a computer needs technology to access the world wide web, or a radio needs crystals or a satellite to receive waves, the electro-magnetic pattern of the human mind needs to reach a certain frequency in order to connect with the vast Universal Consciousness.

In large meditation gatherings, each individual being that is merging with the whole, ends up purifying and expanding their own mind as well as upgrading the magnetic frequency of their thought patterns. These gatherings produce a tangible heart-opening. A One Mind.

Yogi Bhajan said that daily practice done in truthful company will always have this effect; some great benefits of meditating in the group energy field are the experience of "mind expansion", love, connectedness, and compassion. This is why Yogi Bhajan gave us group meditations such as the Aquarian Sadhana and the White Tantric Yoga events as well as the bi-yearly yoga-centric Summer and Winter Solstices in New Mexico and Florida at which we convene.

"Love and Compassion are necessities, not luxuries. Without them humanity cannot survive." - Dalai Lama

The Universal Mind is the vehicle for Compassionate Activism; a form of activism that is rooted in an underlying compassion for all beings. In "normal" activism there is an urge to dehumanize the opponent or to respond to violence with violence. Compassionate activism is a philosophy of creating transformation on a Universal scale; beyond traditional binary paradigms, war logic, and typical social and political hierarchies. Compassionate Activism does not use domination or violence of any kind and strives to use methods like upgrading the thought waves and vibrations of large groups to influence cultural shifts. When large groups of people are active spiritually together, the force of the Universal Mind is unstoppable and unbeatable.

"Nonviolent resistance does resist," he wrote. "It is not a method of stagnant passivity. While the nonviolent resister is passive in the sense that he is not physically aggressive toward his opponent, his mind and emotions are always active, constantly seeking to persuade his opponent that he is wrong. The method is passive physically, but strongly active spiritually. It is not passive non-resistance to evil; it is active nonviolent resistance to evil."

- Dr. Martin Luther King

INHALE SAT

EXHALE NAM

Long Deep Breathing

Relax your chest and shoulders. Mouth closed unless otherwise indicated. INHALE and relax the abdomen and expand it. EXhale... rather than contracting the chest, allow the abdomen to SHrink back IN.

Normally people use ONLY 1/2 - 3/4 qt. of their 6 1/2 qt. lung capacity when they Breathe !!

on the inhale, the muscles of the abdomen will draw down the diaphragm & the downward movement will create a vacuum in the LUNG cavity... air will FLOW into the Lungs.
on the exhale, this pushes UP on the diaphragm creating lung cavity pressure which cause the air to be expelled.

SO MANY FABULOUS BENEFITS !!

Breath of Fire in EGO ERADICATOR pose

The Breath is an in + out evenly balanced Breath through the nose... with NO emphasis on either the inhale OR the exhale. MOUTH is closed unless otherwise INdicated. Eyes closed and focused upwards, everything stays relaxed even though the navel moves BECAUSE of the breath, NOT the other way around.

* cleanses the entire blood supply IN 3 MINutes
* RAISES VOLTAGE OF NERVOUS SYSTEM.

ARMS UP AT A 60 DEGREE ANGLE FINGERS CURLED ONTO PALM

* INCREASES LUNG CAPA-CITY

TO END: INHALE DEEPLY AND BRING ARMS OVERHEAD WITH THE THUMBS TOUCHING. OPEN FINGERS, EXHALE, AND RELAX THE ARMS DOWN

My Favorite way to PLUG IN

The One Minute Breath

SIT IN A meditation Posture. INHALE for 20 seconds, hold for 20 seconds and

EXHALE for 20 seconds.

TIP #3 Give yourself permission to work up to it... maybe start at 10-10-10 and increase bit by bit as it gets more comfortable.

"IF YOU PRACTICE ONE BREATH A MINUTE FOR ELEVEN MINUTES A DAY.... YOU CAN BE IN CONTROL OF YOUR MIND"- YOGI BHAJAN

TIP#1 take 3 minutes to relax and deepen your breath first, or 3 min Breath of Fire TO RELAX. TIP #2 INHALE SLOWLY starting by filling up the LOWER abdomen, the stomach, up to the Lungs and all the way UP the chest. It should take 20 seconds. HOLD it for 20 seconds and then exhale slowly and steadily for 20 seconds. And then INHALE and keep going. DON'T FIGHT IT you need to be relaxed

"The magic part usually frames itself in my head like a question, a phrase, like, 'What should be? What picture should be? Here.' And I don't know if I mean here in my studio, or here in this world. Sometimes, it comes up as, 'What do I want to do? What do I want to make?' But 'What should be?' is a kind of prior thought to letting an image come up. It will happen any time; it happens sometimes just thinking, 'I know what I want to do,' and then starting. I mean, I mess up the canvas as soon as I can with some sort of paint."

Susan Rothenberg, artist

ART OF UPLINKING

"The cosmic mind through your mind, comes to you; it is a channel."

The   Art of Uplinking is connecting ourselves to the Creative Public Access Channel. A creative person is always working on something whether they are in the studio or not; the radio receiver is always turned on. Creativity in Daily Life or in terms of this book, Create Living means that you are consciously listening, seeing, feeling...no matter what you do; being aware of the world around you and inside of you. Dealing with things as they come, managing emotions, practicing a discipline to keep the channels open and clear. Moving the body. Controlling the mind. Nurturing one's sensitivity. Each and every person, artist or not, has their own way. Creativity in daily life is not necessarily in the studio...it's in the living. Remember... the channel to Infinity is through you.

Some people "wait" for inspiration. Some people show up and do the work on a daily basis, inspired or not. There are many schools of thought on this issue. The writer and artist Henry Miller said that artists are working all the time; for him at parties talking with people and in front of the mirror, shaving. For me, it's walking my dogs. With any method, inspired or not, I agree with writer Henry Miller's assessment that you are always doing the invisible prep work and when the time comes, "it's a mere matter of transfer".

What you take from the ethers and download into your reality could be the brightest idea, the most brilliant thesis, the most original and sought-after screenplay, the cure for an incurable disease, a whole symphony from soup to nuts, your next series of paintings, a novel, or a solution for a mathematical problem. You might see in your mind's eye a way to heal a relationship, a complete choreography of a ballet, how to scale a mountain you're planning to climb, the meaning of life, a fully-realized building; in other words, anything may come to you when open and connected to the vast infinite pool of Cosmic Creativity.

The whole thing can come in a flash. Or it can come in dribs and drabs, fragments or ideas. Filmmaker David Lynch said *"An idea comes – and you see it, and you hear it, and you know it…"* What do you do with this idea that comes to you... this idea that is probably coming to other people at the same time who may or may not be as open, aware and receptive as you are?

"We don't do anything without an idea. So they're beautiful gifts. And I always say, you desiring an idea is like a bait on a hook – you can pull them in. And if you catch an idea that you love, that's a beautiful, beautiful day. And you write that idea down so you won't forget it. And that idea that you caught might just be a fragment of the whole – whatever it is you're working on – but now you have even more bait. Thinking about that small fragment – that little fish – will bring in more, and they'll come in and they'll hook on. And more and more come in, and pretty soon you might have a script – or a chair, or a painting, or an idea for a painting." - David Lynch

Here come some Uplinking rules.....

Rule number one: Good-bye ego. There is nothing that is "yours"; whatever you get from the Universe belongs to all of us. You can think of Cosmic Creativity as a Public Access Channel and all you need to do to get on it is to plug in or tune into...or in computer terms, " to uplink". The definition of uplinking is to link from a ground station up to a satellite. Since the word yoga means "to yoke or join" the finite physical world with the infinite great beyond, we are uplinking from our ground station to the cosmic satellite through our practice of yoga and meditation. Infinity or the great "cosmic satellite" also happens to be where all the ideas are.

Rule number two: Understand that your expression is unique. There is only one you. Even thought the ideas may not be yours, it is you who are the vessel through which they are expressed. Since the Law of Creativity is to conceive, flourish and deliver…you just need to figure out how to connect in order to do some creative conceptualization.

Rule number three: Once connected, Keep the channel open. The iconic dancer Martha Graham said:

"There is a vitality, a life force, an energy, a quickening that is translated through you into action, and because there is only one of you in all of time, this expression is unique. And if you block it, it will never exist through any other medium and it will be lost. The world will not have it. It is not your business to determine how good it is nor how valuable nor how it compares with other expressions. It is your business to keep it yours clearly and directly, to keep the channel open. You do not even have to believe in yourself or your work. You have to keep yourself open and aware to the urges that motivate you. Keep the channel open."

A good practice would be to quiet the ego, connect with Cosmic Conscious, The Creative Flow, Universal Mind (whatever you want to call it - the channel is still the same) and to consciously work on removing your obstacles and dismantling blocks with practicing certain mantras and meditations specific to these issues. The point here is to make the connection because creativity is all about connection.

"Creativity is just connecting things. When you ask creative people how they did something, they feel a little guilty because they didn't really do it, they just saw something. It seemed obvious to them after a while"
—Steve Jobs

OBSTACLES AND INTUITION

Many people I've worked with say *"Oh, but I'm not creative…I can't even draw a straight line!"* Do you really think that drawing a straight line is an indication of being creative? Quite the opposite, actually! Every single one of us is creative because we are all, by nature creative beings. Born to make connections between each other, between ideas, between energy fields, we are perfect and "in the flow" when we are born. For one reason or another, we shut ourselves down as we get older; sometimes to fit in, sometimes to avoid being judged. When our feelings get hurt we close down the connection a little more. Society is always trying to dumb us down, put out our iconoclastic fire. Little by little, we cultivate negative habits like negative self-talk and we wonder why we feel stuck. We believe the advertisers when they tell us we are not complete and buy their products to feel whole.

We get to a certain point in our lives and we realize that we want to be happier, to experience more joy, love, prosperity, and creativity in our lives. We want to make more heart-felt connections. When you are creative, you are living as you were meant to be. Yogi Bhajan said that the Creative Flow is the purpose of life. So let's get out of our own way and use intuition to get there!

"Person with an intuition can run the obstacle race for life because each time when an obstacle comes, he goes over it. He doesn't waste time, energy and does not get involved with it emotionally, commotion- ally, does not tie it and he is not bonded with it - he goes over it. So that way, you reach a standard of life. There are three things in life which are very important. You, your caliber and your standard."

As an artist, educator and consultant, I have seen so many people spend gargantuan amounts of time and energy on being "stuck". Some of my favorite things to teach in my high school and college art classes are creative tricks and tools so that students never have to experience artists' block. In yoga classes, I find that so many students come to class feeling blocked, shut down, overwhelmed and stuck. Because there are so many ways to get out of it using both art "tricks" and Kundalini Yoga technology, I find that the main reason people stay stuck is because they choose to. Anyone can use these creative and yogic tools to get a better "uplink" in order to get the flow going or to go over the obstruction ...that is, if they want to.

The most important thing about creativity that I tell art students is the importance of using their intuition; that there is no right or wrong when it comes to creativity. It's all about flexibility. All the artistic intelligence, talent and experience in the world won't get you unstuck... but intuition will. Creativity is about thinking that anything is possible in any given circumstance and having the intuitive fluidity of mind and the courage to invent, experiment and project. When they get out of their own heads about wanting to look like creative geniuses, they actually do great work. Sometimes an "accident" can occur that turns out to be a stroke of pure genius...but you have to have the intuitive achievement and the energy in order to know whether or not to use it. This is one of my absolute favorite quotes that I always give to my art students:

"There are many accidents that are nothing but accidents - and forget it. But there are some that were brought about only because you are the person you are... you have the wherewithal, intelligence, and energy to recognize it and do something with it." - Helen Frankenthaler, artist

I tell them, when you are "stuck" and don't know what to do, you just have to start. You just have to do something. In fact there are 5 Sutras of the Aquarian Age that Yogi Bhajan gave to us that address this very issue: The second sutra is "There is a way through every block" and the third sutra is "When the time is on you, start, and the pressure will be off. "

For example, I tell painting students that they can always do something. They can always paint or draw what they see; a self-portrait for example, or a still life of the items around them. They can switch it up and make something with their non-dominant hand. They can give themselves a certain amount of time to just sit quietly with eyes closed, breathe deeply and then sketch what they feel or see. Or they can move around, dance, or walk. There's always something you can do to move energy and each project doesn't have to be the Sistine Chapel. In yoga classes I always say "this is not a yoga performance, this is a yoga practice" and I pretty much feel the same way about art.

If you are a writer, you can do automatic writing or talk into your smartphone and transcribe it. No matter what your creative discipline, you can always do something different. If you are a musician, dance. If you are a photographer, bake a cake. There is not a thing in the world that is not a creative act, so anything you do will have the same effect of getting the energy to move. When the time is on you, start, and the pressure will be off. The point being that it doesn't really matter WHAT you do, just do something. If you move your body, you'll move the energy and in turn, you'll move your mind.

Yogi Bhajan said that how you handle your obstacles will give you the standard of your life. What is your standard of life? He explains:

"Some people are very rich, they will never dress up, they will never eat right, they just drag their heels. There are some people who are very poor, they are neat, clean, absolutely to the point. So there is a caliber and there is a standard and there is you. These three things are essential... everybody's faculty of caliber is based on everybody's intuitive achievement."

And just to be clear, intuition is the cosmic mind coming through your mind.

If you can turn obstacles into games and blocks into opportunities for creative action, then the universe is at your command and you are raising the standard of your life. In order to do that, you need to strengthen your intuition which is governed by the third eye; the sixth chakra.

Yogi Bhajan said that intuition is based on *"the relationship, between man's pineal and man's pituitary, in psycho electric magnetic field, at the rate of frequency, which is connected at theta level, with the entire universe One way is, you are subjected to the universe, the other way, is universe is your subject."*

The problem is that even though the blockage may seem valid at first, we will analyze it, cherish it, and fortify it until it becomes an even bigger block. Some people put all their energy and creativity into being blocked instead of putting all their energy and creativity into removing it. I'm not saying that all obstacles or blocks are imaginary, but many of them are and you can dismantle, vaporize, go around or go over them. It just takes some self-love.

"This my life, your life, our life, and this life has only one problem, you can be blocked. Block is always square. If you cut the square diagonally, that's the tantric energy, you will have two triangles and triangle is a sign of prosperity. Block is a sign of obstacle. Now, try to understand in your life, when you are blocked and you start loving a block, then, that block becomes your deity, it becomes your energy, it becomes your Goddess, it becomes your worship, it becomes your altar and altar has no alternative. So basically, you create a block and a block and a block and a block finally, you create a wall and you don't move. Breaking the block is loving the self."

So, if you stay inside your self-built wall, you are essentially not loving yourself; you stand in the way from having a more loving and creative relationship with your self and everything and everyone around you. Why not use your innate creativity to get over the wall? Remember these three things: Your caliber is your basic, consistent power that you use to project who you are, communicate who you are, and lodge yourself, like a bullet, in whatever you do.

Your standard is HOW you choose to break through or go over your obstacles. And you is you; your identity, your Sat Nam.

By staying blocked you create a situation or an identity crisis. We all know how much attention we can get if we go that route. Your choice is to either create a sovereign identity or you can create an identity crisis; you can create powerful positive trends in your life or you can create disaster and corruption. Both come out of the Creative Flow but how we direct the energy is up to us.

Here's the great thing about intuition: you can either muscle through a block or your can strengthen your intuition. If you muscle through by using your mind and your creativity, that's a great option and certainly one you'll be called on to use again and again in your life so that is a great skill to master. But to get to the root cause, you need to develop your intuition which will not only vaporize obstacles, but will prevent you from building walls out of them. Chances are, they won't come back. The universe can be at YOUR command and you can do this by working with the higher chakras, in particular the sixth chakra (the third eye).

The sixth chakra is located in the brain, at the brow point above the base of the nose and it is from this energy center, also called the Ajna chakra, that the major channels of energy (the ida, the pingala and the shushmuna) all come together. Because of this, Ajna which means "to command", allows you mastery over the duality and the flow of your mind. The gift is the direct link between your mind and the Universe.

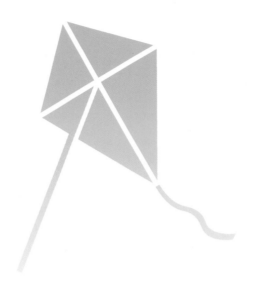

PRACTICAL GUIDE TO UPLINKING

"You can never have flexibility without an intuitive mind. You can't cope with anything because to cope with something is the mind, and if mind cannot change gears, you can't catch up with speed."

Meditation is necessary.

You must meditate to train and discipline the mind because it has the faculty to analyze everything in the shortest amount of time. This faculty is called intuition. Physical exercise is necessary. You must move the body with yoga that preferably will make you sweat. This will strengthen your mind, control your passions and ego and give you the physical and nervous system strength to hold things in balance; to hold the electromagnetic charge of a commitment. *Pranayam* (breath exercises) are necessary. You must breathe consciously in order to connect with your neutrality. Your neutrality allows you to speak and act from your intuition. Mantra is necessary. You must have a go-to mantra that can connect you with the infinite in you which will teach you how to listen.

Yogi Bhajan said *"The greatest tool you have in your life is to listen. Why? If you listen, you will listen sensitively. And you will be shocked how fast you will become intuitive."*

When you practice these things on a daily basis, you will find that everything you do can be connected to that infinite source. You can connect to the "satellite", but you must develop the energy and nervous system strength to sustain the connection. It is your business to stay in awareness and keep the channel open.

"Searching for music is like searching for God. They're very similar. There's an effort to reclaim the unmentionable, the unsayable, the un-seeable, the unspeakable, all those things, comes into being a composer and to writing music and to searching for notes and pieces of musical information that don't exist." – David Bowie

There are so many great Kundalini Yoga meditations and pranayama too numerous to mention here in this volume, that will boost your intuition. I mentioned the One Minute Breath in the Universal Mind chapter - that breathing exercise is my personal favorite. Or just breathe consciously. You can do that anytime and anywhere.

A conscious breath is inhaling as long and as deep as you can and then exhaling as much as you can. I also like the Four-stroke Breath to Build Intuition that I've included in the back of this chapter.

Art-making in itself can open your intuition. Here are four essential guidelines for this kind of practice:

1) Be here now…you must be in the moment. Do not think about what it is going to look like when its done or what someone else may think of it. Do not think about artwork you've done in the past or artwork you might do in the future.

2) Practice conscious observation. Be aware of everything around you and in you. Every sound, every smell. In this way, your art-making becomes a meditative act.

3) Become one with the Process. The process itself is an act of self-discovery and a quieting of the ego. Try not to judge what you are doing. Like automatic writing, you just move the pen or pencil across the page without editing as you go.

4) Intuition. Go with your gut. Go with the flow. Listen to your inner voice. Activate your sensitivity by listening to your self. Only stop working when you are happy; when you feel the inner completion. You will find a pathway or a channel that you can return to again and again. And just like a muscle, the more you use it, the stronger it will get. When we mistrust our intuition, we get into trouble. When we trust our intuition, the world is laid out before us in perfect order. Uplinking is nothing more than activating your intuitive powers through the activation of the third eye; your sixth chakra.

"Intuition is the outcome of the sixth chakra. And intuition is the source of happiness. Intuition is the personal reality to which your personality has to adjust. The natural beauty that you will like to flow in your life in a normal way will come out of your intuition. It won't come out of your intelligence, because in your intelligence, rarely will you use the neutral mind. When your ego works, intuition doesn't; when your intuition works, ego doesn't."

"Practice listening to your intuition, your inner voice; ask questions; be curious; see what you see; hear what you hear; and then act upon what you know to be true. These intuitive powers were given to your soul at birth."

Clarissa Pinkola Estés, writer

Remember the three rules I mentioned at the beginning of this chapter? Let's review:

1) Get the ego out of the creativity equation... there is nothing that is "yours" anyway; whatever you get from the Universe belongs to all of us. What you are uplinking to is public access!

2) Understand that your expression is unique. There is only one you.

3) and once connected, keep the channel open

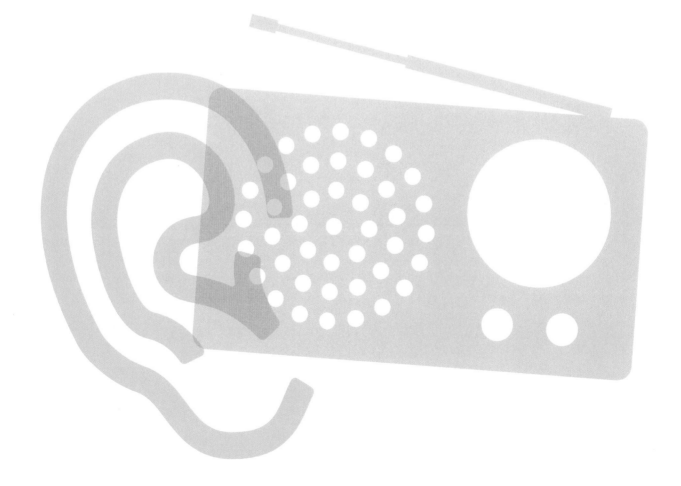

"WHAT IS AN ARTIST? THEY ARE A PERSON WHO HAS ANTENNAE, WHO KNOWS HOW TO HOOK UP TO THE CURRENTS WHICH ARE IN THE ATMOSPHERE, IN THE COSMOS; THEY MERELY HAVE THE FACILITY TO "HOOKING ON", AS IT WERE.

WHO IS ORIGINAL? EVERYTHING THAT WE ARE DOING, EVERYTHING THAT WE THINK EXISTS ALREADY, AND WE ARE ONLY INTERMEDIARIES, THAT'S ALL, WHO MAKE USE OF WHAT IS IN THE AIR. WHY DO IDEAS, WHY DO GREAT SCIENTIFIC DISCOVERIES OFTEN OCCUR IN DIFFERENT PART OF THE WORLD AT THE SAME TIME? THE SAME IS TRUE OF THE ELEMENTS THAT GO TO MAKE UP A POEM OR A GREAT NOVEL OR ANY WORK OF ART. THEY ARE ALREADY IN THE AIR, THEY HAVE NOT BEEN GIVEN VOICE, THAT'S ALL. THEY NEED THE PERSON, THE INTERPRETER, TO BRING THEM FORTH."

HENRY MILLER, PARIS REVIEW

FOUR-STROKE BREATH to BUILD INTUITION

CONTINUE FOR UP TO 16 MINUTES

Place your hands together in prayer mudra. Keep jupiter fingers (index) extended as you interlock the other fingers to clasp your 2 hands together. CROSS the THUMBS.

Make your eyes 9/10 closed. Place the mudra a little below your nose where you can LOOK at the tips of your fingers (jupiter) through the 1/10 opening of your eyes.
INHALE is 4 powerful strokes through the "O" mouth. 1 stroke per second = 4 second inhale. AND Exhale in One powerful stroke through the Nose (1 sec)

to finish... sit straight, inhale, hold your breath 20 Seconds + stretch your arms out to the Side, palms facing upwards. That will give you poweR to balance your central spinal column. EXHALE. Inhale deep, hold your breath 20 seconds & stretch arms horizontally & stretch the spine vertically. Make A T-square. EXHALE. Inhale deep hold your breath 20 seconds and OPEN UP your fingers, make them like STEEL.

SQUEEZE
your entire
energy &
Bring it INTO
your ARMS.
EXHALE.........and relax

"To receive, to conceive, and to deliver, it's natural."

Yogi Bhajan

ART OF CONCEIVING

THE NUCLEUS OF CREATIVITY

To receive is uplinking to the the Creative Flow; the public access cosmic creativity channel. After that comes the conceive part where what you pull into your consciousness takes root; like what David Lynch means when he gets fragments of ideas and then those fragments attract more fragments to make a whole. Steve Jobs said that creativity is just connecting things. In other words, when the ideas come, you have to make sense of them in some manner and allow for them to implant, connect and synthesize.

The word conceive basically means "to form" but has its origins in the old French conceivre which comes from the Latin word concipere "to take fully or to take in". One can take in an idea or an opinion in the mind but can also conceive a child in the body. A woman receives, conceives and delivers in order to give birth to a child and this great creative act is no different than any other creative enterprise.

To conceive implies that the idea or creative inspiration comes from elsewhere. This is a very important point.

"There is a void in every life. There is a void in every life of a unfulfilled being. How can he be fulfilled? He can be fulfilled if he understands and tries ... to realize Infinity. And how to realize Infinity? The Infinity can only be realized through

one idea only -if you make your thought wave into
a idea. There is nothing more powerful on this planet,
than an idea Idea is something, which is beyond you
and which you have grabbed. That's called idea..... I-d-
ea. The sound of word idea is very simple sound. And
what is that idea? That I am the part of the
Infinity. Think, feel, do everything in that shape and
form, you will be happiest person"

So, according to Yogi Bhajan, an idea, being something that you have to
grab from somewhere beyond you, must have fertile ground in which to
implant. It is necessary for you to be in a receptive state which comes
from opening the energy channels, strengthening the nervous system,
and diminishing the ego interference.

By cultivating awareness, radiance and intuition, you prepare yourself so
that you can recognize what is "out there" that can be of use to you. All
of this prepares your body, mind and spirit so that the "idea", once
implanted can take root in your consciousness and grow.

SENSITIVITY AND COMMITMENT

The Art of Conceiving is a creative person's natural gift but anyone,
through practice, can improve one's ability to conceive. We become
better conceivers through the deepening and nurturing of our
sensitivity and commitment.

"Creativity and love come from your sensitivity. A
developed sensitivity in character gives you
commitment. Commitment in turn gives you more
sensitivity of character. They are interrelated. That
is how this planet runs."

We need the sensitivity to recognize the thought waves and the commitment to transform them into ideas. **Why is commitment so important in creativity?** Because commitment is the energy that will eventually bring the idea into reality. Commitment is knowledge within itself. Committing won't get you the knowledge, but when you commit, the knowledge will come to you. So part of the preparation for conceiving the idea, or a baby for that matter, is the commitment energy behind it. In creativity, you get a hunch and if that hunch has some tack, you'll stick to it and as Yogi Bhajan said,

"if you can commit and stick with it, there is nothing more you have to learn. When you commit, things will happen which will shift in you, change you, stop you, may tempt you to disobey, revolt. Such opportunities will come to you. Even if you forget the truth that is the basis of you, if you continue to be committed, that's all it takes. Commitment does not 'begin' anything. Commitment is the end in itself."

The Law of Creativity is driving both the conscious conception of a child and the conscious conception of an idea. The conception phase is very exciting for me; it feels a lot like the atmosphere right before it's going to rain - the liminal electromagnetic space between the air pressure and the first lightening strike–- just prior to the first raindrop. It's that moment in which you know that all the energy in the air is going to manifest into to something wet and wonderful.

It's intoxicating!

"I don't know what the work is going to look like. I know what it's going to feel like. I know what I want people to feel then they go into that space, and then it's just a matter of finding that visual language. I'm in the midst of all of these blank-ish, red, cadmium red canvases, but I know that they're getting ready to burst into being or to become something. This is the conception phase. - Kenyatta A.C. Hinkle, interdisciplinary artist, performer, writer

THE NUCLEUS OF CREATIVITY...IT REALLY IS A NUCLEUS

You can't talk about the excitement and anticipation of the conception phase of creativity without talking about the feel-good neurotransmitter and hormone, dopamine. It is released by the brain when we satisfy cravings, or when we have sex, or basically any activity that contributes to our pleasure and satisfaction. You can think of the release of dopamine as a neuro-chemical reward that boosts your motivation and makes commitment easier because it increases your focus and attention and thus enabling you to stay on track. In all those lab experiments, it's the dopamine that prompts a rat to press the lever for food over and over again. Humans act just like the rats and that is why addiction is so prevalent among us.

We love the feeling that dopamine gives us just before something we think might make us feel good is going to happen. The caudate nucleus, which is involved in the anticipation of pleasure, seeps dopamine just before peak moments of cognition or emotional resonance… just like for me, before it starts raining, which is why it makes me so happy.

Dopamine is not the only neurotransmitter involved in creativity; serotonin is the other. Baba Shiv, a marketing professor at Stanford's Graduate School of Business (whose research focuses on the role neural structures play in decision making and economic behavior) is especially intrigued by the biological roots of creativity. According to his findings, creativity resides at the intersection of two primary pathways in the brain. On one pathway, serotonin is responsible for whether you are operating from a sense of calm or from a position of anxiety and fear. On the other pathway, dopamine is responsible for your anticipatory excitement and engagement rather than apathy and boredom.

For most creatives, neurologically speaking of course, a high level of both serotonin and dopamine would be ideal thus enabling you to be calm and energized at the same time. And arriving in this blissfully creative state where your hormones and neurotransmitters are in perfect balance, is the reason we are doing Kundalini Yoga to support creativity.

A big effect of Kundalini yoga is how it heals our nervous systems; balancing the parasympathetic (which calms you) and sympathetic (which excites and alerts you) nervous systems. A effective meditation to engage your "chill out response" would be to listen to the gong.

Understanding how the brain works during the process of creativity, which can be incredibly exciting in this conception phase, might encourage you to meditate and make art more often; both of which increase pleasure and connect you to the flow of creativity. Since the caudate nucleus acts like an antenna that receives and transmits frequencies, it is a useful tool for telepathy and contacting the Universal Mind, downloading cosmic knowledge and is thought to have the ability to act as the Higher Self's microphone and speaker.

Doesn't it look like a headset of one of those bluetooth devices you slip behind your ear?

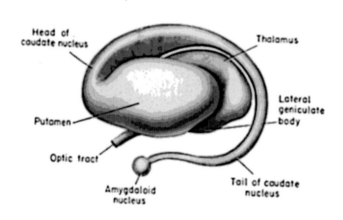

And aside from all this wonderful juicy paranormal stuff, it is mostly known as the part of brain responsible for learning and memory. But wait, there's more!

It is said, when activated, the caudate nucleus is capable of bi-location, telekinesis, remote viewing, zapping viruses, bacteria, fungi, and parasites; neutralizing harmful electromagnetic frequencies and toxins, clairvoyance, and teleportation!!!!! Sounds like the job description of the aura!

In 2006, a neuroscientist from the University of Montreal put out a call for volunteer nuns "who have had an experience of intense union with God " in order to answer the question, *Is There a God Spot in the Brain?*

In his Scientific American article, *Searching for God in the Brain* David Biello writes about these nun experiments:

"The researchers found six regions that were invigorated only during the nuns' recall of communion with God. The spiritual memory was accompanied by, for example, increased activity in the caudate nucleus, a small central brain region to which scientists have ascribed a role in learning, memory and, recently, falling in love; the neuroscientists surmise that its involvement may reflect the nuns' reported feeling of unconditional love."

MEDITATION FOR THE NEUTRAL ~ MIND ~

IT'S EASY TO HEAR A TRUTH AND DIFFICULT TO LIVE IT, TO EMBED IT DEEPLY INTO YOUR HEART AND MIND. THE NEUTRAL MIND OPENS THE GATE TO THAT DEEP Remembrance OF THE SELF and SOUL.

THE NEUTRAL MIND LIVES FOR THE TOUCH OF VASTNESS. IT LETS ALL OTHER THoughts be WITHOUT Disturbance to your Constant inner light.

Call on the higher Self and keep going steadily through all barriers. Let Go and let God.

Practice this meditation for 11-31 minutes at a session.

SIT IN EASY POSE WITH THE SPINE STRAIGHT. PUT BOTH HANDS IN THE LAP WITH THE PALMS FACING UP. REST THE RIGHT HAND INTO THE LEFT. THE THUMBTIPS MAY TOUCH OR NOT. Remove all tension FROM every Part of the Body. Sit straight by achieving a balance. CLOSE THE EYES. Imagine seeing yourself sitting peacefully and FULL OF Radiance. Then gradually let your energy collect like a flow at the Browpoint. Let the Breath regulate itself into a slow...meditative, almost Suspended manner. Concentrate without effort at that POINT and mentally VIBRATE IN a simple monotone, as IF CHOPPING the SOUND, projecting Each syllable DISTINCTLY:

WHA-HAY GU-ROO

INFINITY IDENTITY FROM DARKNESS TO LIGHT

ART OF CONCEIVING HIGHLIGHTS

1. Yogi Bhajan's Law of Creativity is to Conceive, Flourish and Deliver.

2. To conceive implies that the idea or "creative inspiration" comes from elsewhere.

3. At the act of creative conception, you are (as if) instantly transforming a thought wave into an idea.

4. You need fertile ground in which to implant so that means healthy receptivity. Keep your energy channels and the creative flow open, strengthen the nervous system, and work on diminishing ego. interference.

5. Sensitivity in character will give you commitment and commitment in turn gives you more sensitivity of character. They are interrelated and crucial to understanding the Art of Conceiving.

6. Commitment is SO IMPORTANT! Even though it seems to appear to us at the beginning of the process, it does not start anything. Commitment is the end in itself.

7. The Law of Creativity is driving both the conscious conception of a child and the conscious conception of an idea.

8. The Art of Conceiving will give you the experience of magic happening; partly because it produces a neuro-chemical reward in the brain, but mostly because it's the start of something BIG.

The Art of Conceiving is a very important and pleasurable part of Creative Living - it is where the pure magic happens. Artists like to be there because it's just before you start working on your project in this reality and there is so much possibility, anticipation and yes…the feel-good brain chemicals, too. As a creative person, when you don't know what is going to happen but you have the commitment in place to go forward it is literally like jumping out of an airplane without a parachute. And for many people, especially performers, that being or conceiving in the moment is the feeling they love they most. For others, it can be the most terrifying.

"You can practice to learn a technique, but I'm more interested in conceiving of something in the moment."

- Herbie Hancock, musician

ART OF

FLOURISHING

ORGANIZING AND PRODUCING IN A HEALTHY WAY

"To practice any art, no matter how well or badly is a way to make your soul grow. SO DO IT." Kurt Vonnegut, writer

What a great word flourish is! The dictionary meaning of flourish is to grow or develop in a healthy or vigorous way, especially as the result of a particularly favorable environment; to thrive, prosper, or bloom; or to announce with fanfare and embellishment.

To flourish is also a great state of being. In Kundalini Yoga, flourishing is usually the outcome of practicing on a regular basis whether or not "flourishing" was your original intention. It's being in the flow and making good use of it. When negative thought forms and behaviors drop off and not-so-promoting habits are replaced with much more promoting ones we can't help but be filled with positive creative energy. The outcome is likely to be contentment, fearlessness, expansive thinking and being, healthy production, prosperity in all its forms, and happiness. True happiness.

Flourishing is the state of being in which you are living creatively; it's the prosperity and the love in your life doing it's fabulous thing while you are wherever you are, doing whatever it is that you do.

```
"I have conceived the idea. I am pregnant with it. And
I deliver the resultant of my idea of conception and
my maintenance of it, the pregnancy. Between the two
lines, the diagonal is the delivery and I want it. I
have found I am in absolute control and everything
around me is going to serve me."
```

Basically, the flourishing phase is the pregnancy of your creation and if you live creatively, then your whole life is like an ongoing pregnancy with the glorious anticipation of infinite deliveries. The deliveries manifest as sharing, impacting others, and transmuting, like an alchemist, the subtle unformed energies into tangibles that can be experienced by all.

Creativity is misunderstood as a thing that only special people possess, and while talent may be the result of a gift or extensive practice, the creative flow is available to everyone. In the previous chapters, I talked about uplinking to the Universal Consciousness aka the Cosmic Creative Flow and conceiving and implanting ideas that were originally received as thought waves.

These sequences take us to the Art of Flourishing; where all the implanted ideas start to grow and bear fruit. As thrilling as the conception phase can be, the flourishing phase is grounded in work, nurturing, research, building, organizing and producing; all in a healthy way.

Your Kundalini energy is your creative flow... and through your practice of Kundalini Yoga and meditation, the ongoing result is the experience that you are creating a life in which you have something of value to share. It may take the form of art, or commerce, or healing, or even how you relate to the people in your life. No matter how this flow manifests in your world, the byproduct is this glorious flourishing phase and as a result, your life goes from ordinary to extraordinary in a very short amount of time.

THE SUPERPOWER TO MAKE SOMETHING OUT OF NOTHING

"Vision without execution is hallucination." -Thomas Edison

Yogi Bhajan had described the word G.O.D. as an acronym for the basic forces of the universe that control pure consciousness: Generating, Organizing and Destroying/Delivering. These energies reside in you and everywhere around you; whenever you generate/conceive, organize/flourish, and deliver/destroy, you are a mirror of the entire universe in action. The Law of Creativity and G.O.D. are inter-changeable, are the basis of creating life, and the basis of making art. Any way you look at it, this force is so strong within you that when it wants to be awakened, you have to pay attention. We all know how babies are born; when you are making art, similarly you conceive an idea, it blossoms and grows within you and then you deliver or put it out into the world. Flourishing is nurturing the idea and manifesting it so that it can join our material reality.

"A definition of art is that it makes concrete our most subtle emotions." - Eva Hesse, artist

If the Art of Conceiving requires commitment, then the Art of Flourishing requires focused production - sometimes bordering on obsession. The flourish part of the law of creativity is when you get to work it out; to feed it and watch it grow. It takes an insatiable appetite for self-discovery with a healthy dose of stubbornness. You have to stay "on it" in order to ready it for delivery. Eternal vigilance is another good description of the kind of energy you need for this flourishing phase.

"Don't only practice your art, but force your way into its secrets; art deserves that, for it and knowledge can raise man to the Divine." - Ludwig Van Beethoven

Like Beethoven said, you have to go deep and this takes courage, faith, stamina and laser-like focus. It would serve you well to practice yoga and meditation that strengthened your navel center and boosted your electromagnetic field. During this phase, you need to create new promoting habits, access your passion, and produce enough energy to get to work.

Cooking a meal for a loved one is as elevated an art form and spiritual pursuit as music, dance, theatre, visual arts, and/or writing. So is parenting or being in a relationship, which actually requires more creativity and spirituality than designing sacred architecture. Teaching is basically a performative art and requires the patience of a saint..just sayin'. Art and spirituality are so interrelated that it's almost impossible to separate them. There is an important element in both art and spirituality which is important to mention;

they both require the insatiable drive to know more, to go deeper, to find truth. Soul searching is a big part of it and like pearl-diving, it's harder for some than for others. And as with pearl diving, only the ones who can handle the pressure come out with the prize in hand.

"I usually work in a direction until I know how to do it, then I stop. At the time that I am bored or understand - I use those words interchangeably - another appetite has formed. A lot of people try to think up ideas. I'm not one. I'd rather accept the irresistible possibilities of what I can't ignore." - Robert Rauschenberg, artist

NAVEL ALCHEMY

Back to yoga...in order to maintain this state of flourishing, one must transform and utilize energies that originate in what is called the "lower triangle". The lower triangle consists of the first three chakras or energy centers. The first chakra is located at the base of the spine and it's energy deals with survival issues and instinct, security, habits, and self-acceptance. This feeling of "grounded-ness" that a balanced first chakra can provide is essential for success on every level.

The second chakra is located in the sex organs and it's energy deals with issues of feeling, desire, creativity and merging. Artist blocks or procrastination usually occur when there is a blockage in these two lowest chakras. Any creative person will tell you that when this happens, it's a living hell. Feeling stuck makes you feel even MORE desperate, more insecure, more worried, and completely undisciplined. And then, you might find that you make unhealthy choices that might not be in your best interest; and probably the worst one for a creative person is giving up.

For example, if you are feeling unsupported because of financial challenges, this might trigger a block because worry and fear diminishes your energy. You can nurture the negative feelings and thoughts inside of your stagnation OR you can generate more energy, take action and move the location of your thoughts. Remember a few chapters back…."wherever you will plug your mind, that you shall be".

"The way to create art is to burn and destroy ordinary concepts and to substitute them with new truths that run down from the top of the head and out of the heart." - Charles Bukowski, poet

The third chakra, at the navel point or solar plexus, is the center of the will, personal power and commitment. When a person is blocked or low in energy here, they are out of balance and it is hard for them to move forward. The lack of confidence from this imbalance prevents the delivery of an idea or project or creates confusion as to which direction to go. So if you are feeling stuck or confused, one of the ways to move forward is to generate and balance the energy in the third chakra. Once you do that, you will have enough power to move and transform the energies in the lower chakras so that they can move into the heart, the throat, the third eye, the crown and into the aura then you will have a situation where your whole self is creating, balancing and maintaining this divine state of flourishing.

Sometimes you might require a total reboot and that might require a bit of extra work; you might have to increase your yoga and meditation practice, go to the studio more, work a little harder, put in more time and energy. Some times it seems to re-boot on its own and therefore, appears to effortlessly shift into a higher gear. In both cases, try to stay in awareness of the process. **The Art of Flourishing is all about the process.**

"...these words were just streaming out and there were tears running down my face. But I couldn't stop, they just flew out. It's an odd feeling, like something else is guiding you, although forcing your hand is more like it." - David Bowie

So provided you've swallowed the bitter pill about the source and ownership of ideas - that an idea is something which is beyond you and that which you have grabbed - You should ask yourself these questions, considering your circumstances and what it would take to bring the "idea" into fruition:

1) *how can I create balance around it's development and delivery?*

2) *Will it create an impact?*

3) *and if so, what kind of impact do I want it to have?*

4) *How can I be of service to this idea so that it will have the impact I desire?*

The Art of Flourishing, essentially being "the pregnancy" or process of an idea or a project; it is where you do your organizing, balancing, and energy building. It's a wonderful stage because you can see the work take shape and you develop a relationship with it and it takes on a life of its own.

"In life, the third chakra is yes and no. High and low is balanced at the third chakra. It is a point of pure energy. If you do not know to balance the third chakra, you may have all the degrees, all the knowledge, all the money, all the beauty, but you shall be unhappy. Because it is not what you feel, it is not what you know, it is not what you can do-it is how you can balance it. When you cannot balance, you cannot live".

The third chakra or the navel point, has a special relationship with chanting mantra, too. When you speak a mantra using the tongue and then bring awareness to the central channel of your spine (*shushmuna*) and use the power of your navel, this trifecta will move the words into the realm of anahat, considered by yoga masters to be the ultimate state of mind. It can bring you great intuition and tremendous inner strength. Once we connect with and fully awaken the energies of the first three chakras, the bigger picture of Self begins to emerge.

"Creativity is contagious ....pass it on"

Albert Einstein

MANTRAS FOR CREATIVITY

You don't have to know the meaning of a mantra, but it's essential to know the correct pronunciation and the rhythm. In many Kundalini Yoga kriyas, instructions are given to copy the sound of a mantra; to chant along even if one doesn't know the words. Just copying the sound current as you hear it can not only create the necessary vibrations for positive transformation, but will teach you the mantra on both a conscious and cellular level.

Chanting mantra creates vibrations in the body and in the brain; these vibrations cause neurolinguistic effects which can induce altered states of consciousness. When the meaning of a mantra is known, then psycho-linguistic effects can be utilized in order to achieve certain goals. They imprint themselves on the subconscious mind and re-wire the neurotransmitters in the brain.

Mantras have intense physical benefits such as regulating brain chemistry, blocking stress hormones and releasing endorphins. They regulate the heart rate, increase immune functions and lower blood pressure. Mantras replace negative thoughts with positive sound current, ease fear and promote relaxation, and suppress obsessive self-destructive tendencies. They also can re-direct the mind in very specific and beneficial ways. One of the ways you can use mantra is to access and manage the creative flow in this extremely crucial flourishing stage in order to get ready for the next stage, delivery.

Some Mantras Effective for Accessing and Managing Creativity

Har

* *one of the aspects of God - the seed sound of creativity and prosperity - Infinite creativity manifest*

Ong Sohung

* *To get out if "I" and "we" to go into "thou". Ong means creative consciousness and hung stimulates and opens the Heart Chakra.*

Har har har har gobinday, Har har har har mukunday

Har har har har udaaray, Har har har har apaaray

Har har har har hareeung, Har har har har kareeung

Har har har har nirnaamay, Har har har har akaamay

* *Fixes the mind to prosperity and power and contains the 8 facts of self. Har is the original force of Creativity. It converts fear into determination and brings all the powers to serve your true purpose.*

Adi Shakti Namo namo

Sarab shaktee namo namo

Pritham bhaagavatee, namo namo

Kundalinee, maataa shaktee, namo namo

- *Invokes the primary Creative power which is manifest as the feminine or Divine Mother.*

- *It takes away insecurities and gives you a deep understand of the cosmic forces and consciousness.*

Aad such jugged such hai BHAY such Nanak hosee BHAY such

- *This is effective for artist block as it means "all that is stuck shall move". It adds the seeds of prosperity and creativity into your personality.*

Har Haray haree wa he guru

- *This mantra combines shakti (power) with bhakti (devotion) which expresses the three qualities of creativity: seed, flow, and completion. It also can bring prosperity as well as creativity and can bring your through any block in life*

Ek ong Kaar (uh)

Saa-taa-naa-ma (uh)

Siree whaa (uh)

Hay gu-roo

- *The Laya Yoga Kundalini Mantra will make you creative and focused on your real priorities and purpose*

- *It will give you the experience of your true identity and is the key to unlocking the realm of creative sound. (see full write up in the chapter on Blueprint for Creativity)*

"IT DOESN'T MATTER WHAT YOU HAVE OR WHAT YOU DON'T HAVE. IT MATTERS ONLY HOW EASILY YOU CAN LET GO"
YOGI BHAJAN

The state of Flourishing is actively enjoying "the process" and it's also the same as being in the flow of prosperity. Yogi Bhajan said that the best way to explain prosperity is that it's …

"like a rosebud when it flowers and opens up, and shares its fragrance. That's the moment, which lasts a few days, when a rose flower is prosperous. When a man or woman is prosperous, it is the fragrance of security, grace, depth, character and truthfulness that a person can share. Like a candle emits light, a human emits prosperity."

A big characteristic of prosperity is non-attachment - and it's a big characteristic of creativity in the flourishing and delivering stages, too. Create something and share it. Share it with joy, or with the intention of impact, or for creating the vacuum you need to keep creating.

Unfortunately, when many people experience the expansive fragrance of prosperity or are having a productive time in the flourishing stage, they forget that they are experiencing being in the flow. Instead of relaxing into it, they resist, get possessive and then they hold on; sometimes for dear life. Maybe they are worried that it won't be well-received, or maybe someone they're afraid someone will "steal" their idea, or maybe they aren't ready to receive the attention, good or bad for putting it out into the world.

In creative terms, many projects never make it to the delivery stage because of this. Fear always puts a wrench in the works. The whole point of creativity is to share; being attached then, would go against the natural law.

Letting go is the basis of all practices, spiritual, creative or otherwise and without it, delivery is impossible.

The natural law of creativity asks us to be a conduit for infinite energy; whether it passes through us as an embodiment of the teachers that came before us or as pure creative essence. It is our responsibility to prepare to receive it, to conceive it, to nurture and organize it and then to deliver it. All of this requires discipline…even the discipline to relax.

FLOURISHING IS CREATIVE LIVING

Everything you do in your life with awareness becomes a creative act.

There are a million ways to be creative and a million kinds of artists to be; more often than not, when we start to label ourselves, it restricts our expression. That's why in the art world - which loves to label - there is such a thing as a "multi-disciplinary" or "inter-disciplinary" artist. If being an "artist" is being someone who has a particular awareness and the ability to manifest that into a reality that others can respond to in some way, then everyone is an artist.

I love how Chögyam Trungpa describes Dharma Art:

"Dharma art is not purely about art and life alone. It has to do with how we handle ourselves altogether; how we hold a glass of water, how to put it down, how we can hold a note card and make it into a sacred scepter, how we can sit on a chair, how we can work with a table, how we do anything."

In my experience, flourishing is a state of existence that I'd like to be in all the time..I mean, who wouldn't? When you are flourishing, you are much more involved in the process than in the final result. You are super-sensitive and oozing creativity and everything you do in your life is done with a kind of hyper-awareness and it's fun.

Dharma art and Creative Living are concerned more with awareness than with making art. You cannot force this kind of awareness; it has to evolve in a natural and organic way… the result of self-knowledge attained through meditation.

ART OF FLOURISHING HIGHLIGHTS

1. The Art of Flourishing is organizing and producing a vision in a healthy way, being in the creative flow and making good use of it.

2. In order for a plant to go from bud to flower, it needs a certain metabolism or energetic transformation. This is essentially what flourishing is.

3. Flourishing is a process-oriented state of being in which you execute ideas, projects, plans - readying them for delivery.

4. Flourishing is prosperity, love, and creativity doing it's fabulous thing while you are doing whatever it is that you do. Everyone is an artist.

5. Your spiritual and/or creative self-discipline can give you the experience that you are creating a life in which you have something of value to share. Share it and be fearless about it.

6. The Art of Flourishing requires obsessive concentration - create a practice that will give you that one-point focus for energetic determination.

7. The navel center is "Flourishing Central". Understand how the energy works and you will never be without the power needed to execute your projects...and bring them to fruition.

HAR AEROBIC KRIYA

START STANDING UP AND SPREAD YOUR FEET HIP DISTANCE APART

HAR

① BRING YOUR ARMS UP STRAIGHT OVER YOUR HEAD AND CLAP YOUR HANDS TOGETHER 8X CHANTING HAR WITH EACH CLAP.

THIS SET OF EXERCISES SHOULD BE DONE VERY QUICKLY and WITH A FLUID MOTION moving FROM ONE exercise to the NEXT WITHOUT stopping. When DONE Properly, it is a great AEROBIC workout. Repeat the whole sequence 5-6 times. Yogi Bbajan would have the womens'camp attendees do it FOR 62 MINUTES every day !!! Each exercise is 8 beats and on each beat you chant "HAR" using the tip of your tongue + your navel. THIS KRIYA HAS SO MANY POSITIVE BENEFITS!

② BEND OVER FROM THE HIPS AND SLAP THE GROUND 8X CHANTING HAR WITH each SLAP

③ BRING YOUR ARMS OUT TO YOUR SIDES Parallel to the ground, pAlms facing DOWN. The arm movement is about one Foot above and one foot below midline. PUMP your arms up + DOWN 8X chanting HAR.

HAR

HAR

HAR

④ WITH YOUR ARMS STRAIGHT OUT TO THE SIDES YOU WILL JUMP AND CROSS YOUR ARMS IN FRONT OF YOU AND YOUR LEGS AT THE SAME TIME... IN A CRISS-CROSS JUMPING JACK MOTION. CHANT HAR AS YOUR LIMBS CROSS and HAR as they open. 8X chanting HAR.

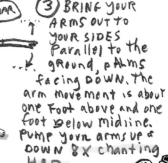

HAR

HAR

⑤ NOW COME INTO ARCHER POSE WITH YOUR RIGHT LEG FORWARD and your left leg BACK CHANTING HAR each time you PULSE FORWARD.... AND BACK... 8X.

⑥ SWITCH SIDES AND DO ARCHER POSE WITH YOUR LEFT Leg FORWARD AND Right leg BACK. PULSE + CHANT HAR 8X

7 Again, same criss-cross jumping exercise as in #4. EIGHT beats of HAR.

8 Stand straight with your arms straight up overhead. Then lean back arcing your back and pulse backwards eight times chanting HAR.

9 Again same criss-cross jumping exercise as in #4. Eight beats of HAR

4X RIGHT   HAR HAR   4X LEFT

10 Stand straight with your arms straight overhead. Then bend to the right pulsing up and DOWN 4 times chanting HAR. SWITCH SIDES AND Bend to your Left side and pulse 4 times chanting HAR

11 Again, same criss-cross jumping exercise as in #4. Eight jumps/beats OF HAR on EACH ONE.

Repeat entire sequence over and over again

ART OF DELIVERANCE

THE RESULT OF ENERGETIC DETERMINATION

"...Ultimately your life depends upon your deliverance. What you deliver, that is what you are. Professionally, personally, individually and systematically. If you cannot deliver goods, you got to go hungry."

As a human being, in order to always rise to the occasion, to take on challenges with grace, to roll with the punches, to have control over your emotions and the direction of your mind, to function well in any given circumstance, to stay positive when the general consensus is negative, to enjoy your life, to see the humor and the magic in most things, to learn from your mistakes and actually make progress toward not repeating them, to be compassionate and kind to everyone, to stay focused on living a healthier and happier life when there are so many distractions, to cultivate courageousness and victory in even the smallest affairs and last but not least, to meet each day with creativity and humility…you must know the technology of how to pull yourself out of inhumanity and your animal nature and discard your attachment to the ego.

In other words, you've got to get your shit together.

The essence of Creative Living is connecting to your own inner consciousness, not the ego. If you connect to the ego, your life will feel like you're dragging around a ton of bricks. If you believe that you are connected to your inner consciousness (G.O.D.), then you won't ever have to feel separate from the source of all things. You may be one of those people who know this and really believe it to be true, yet I am sure that there are times when you feel disconnected and alone. This illusion of separateness is called "maya". Maya tests you, teases you and ultimately if you don't watch out, can destroy you.

If the ego feels like a ton of bricks, then maya is like quicksand. Both ego and maya will pull you down - each in their own way. Ego attachment and maya are a deadly combination, especially for creatives because whatever you've got going on, those two temptresses will take the wind out of your sails. Feeling disconnected from your creative source is a devastating feeling; there's nothing more lonely, more painful and enervating. You are working on a project and you can't seem to stay focused; or there are endless distractions; or you are afraid to release your project into the world for fear of fill-in-the-blank, or you think you can do it better so you avoid completion and so on. This is the work of ego attachment and maya.

So, the question is, why should I be writing about ego and maya in a chapter about The Art of Deliverance? Because if you don't deliver, you will destroy yourself. That's just how it works. Deliverance and destruction are two sides of the same coin and ego and maya are always going to provoke or entice you. That's why I practice Kundalini Yoga; so that I can always keep a few steps ahead of the game... and I want for you to be able to do that, too. Losing touch with your connection to the Creative

Source, or G.O.D. or whatever you want to call it is a very unfortunate situation because then you sink back into the quicksand of delusion.

"Without the guidance, there can be no self-determination. Without self-determination, there can be no achievement. Without achievement, there can be no knowledge. Without knowledge, there can be no awareness. Without awareness, there can be no radiance. And without radiance, you might as well be an animal."

If you want to be successful in your art field, your job, your relationships, or in whatever you do, then you have to ask yourself just how visible, vocal, accessible and active do you want to be? Just remember that you are exactly what you deliver, so whatever you put out there in the world is your very own self-produced advertising campaign.

The Art of Deliverance requires...

1) willpower,
2) self- determination
3) prana and radiance, and
4) the strength and willingness to let go.

These four important skillsets that I'm about to lay out for you will seriously change your life if you utilize them.

So, let's go!

WILLPOWER

In our efforts to move forward, to bring a project to fruition, to see an idea manifest, make good on a promise, we must deliver. All the intentions in the world don't mean anything until you develop your will to ACT.

The dictionary definition of willpower is energetic determination and the will can and must be developed to eclipse the obstacles and bad habits that get in the way of our conscious efforts. How can we have the creative life we want when we can't deliver? Follow-through is as important in creative living as it is in a golf swing. Our deliverance determines what we are and how the world will see us, good or bad. Sometimes we lose steam or we don't know the sequence of steps to take. We all know that subconscious patterns can get in the way of our happiness and success yet we don't take the necessary steps to eliminate them. Why? Because in order to override the old patterns, it takes work. It's just easier to stay where we are.

How many projects have you almost taken to completion only to find yourself producing countless better new endings, getting chronically sidetracked or distracted, or becoming frozen with self-doubt and fear?

As a teaching artist and creativity consultant, I see students and clients with these symptoms of what I call "completion anxiety" all the time. It is not because they lack creativity; in fact, creativity is what they have in spades. What they are lacking, however is the energy needed to take a project all the way to deliverance.

Chögyam Trungpa, Buddhist teacher, scholar and artist said that habit was formed from memory and that it was easier to go back to the past and repeat old patterns than it was to start fresh and "fight our way through foreign territory". It takes hard work and determination to take control of the mind; it's easier to ignore the self than to face the self. A creative person starts out determined with the best intentions, armed to fight through the foreign territory at all costs...but sometimes at the delivery stage, when it's do or die, ego, maya, fear, "completion anxiety"…they all come in to test you. And what you need, plain and simple, is energy.

Conceive, flourish, and deliver. Generate, organize and deliver. No matter how you look at it, the creative power within you is working off of a formula which must be followed and the end result is either delivery or destruction. It's fighting through that "foreign territory", or "forcing your way into the secrets" of a project that ultimately takes you to self-realization. That's why making art is a spiritual pursuit!

In order to bring projects and intentions to completion - to deliver the goods, as it were - it takes pure unadulterated willpower. And believe it or not, self-realization takes willpower, too; it is what you need to go the long haul, to stick to your guns no matter what anybody says or whatever may come along to test or tempt you.

There's a story about Picasso; he was in a cafe and a woman approached him and asked if he would make a little drawing on a napkin for her. He was amused and so obliged and then said "that will be one million dollars". Confused and a bit surprised, she said that it had only taken him thirty seconds to draw! He supposedly responded "No, my dear woman, you are mistaken. It took me thirty years to draw that in thirty seconds!"

Now I wasn't there, so I don't know if it really happened, but it's a good illustration of the kind of willpower one needs to succeed in this world. Willpower, which is the ability to resist short-term gratification for a long-term goal, is what you need to get past the two temptations and distractions of the mind; ego and maya.

"You are what your deep, driving desire is.
As your deep, driving desire is, so is your will.
As your will is, so is your deed.
As your deed is, so is your destiny."
- Upanishads, 800 BCE

SELF-DETERMINATION

The process by which a person controls their own life is self-determination. You have to figure out who you are and what you need to do to be the best you. No one is going to do it for you; no one is going to give you an instruction manual on how to be you. The prescription to be the best me is different than the prescription to be the best you. My life's work is to figure it all out, and if you are reading this book, it's probably your life's work as well.

Self-determination is self-analysis which will lead you to achievement. Without self-analysis, you are just swimming in a sea of feelings. Yogi Bhajan said that you need to ask your self some questions: What do I want? What do I need? What does life mean to me? What do I mean to my life? What kind of environments do I want? What can I do for my environments?

Knowing these things about yourself will give you a special knowledge that you cannot learn any other way than by self- analysis. And knowledge will bring you awareness so you can navigate your life toward more experiences of fulfillment, happiness, creativity, love and prosperity.

When you become aware of who you are, what you want, what you need and so on, you will know your longitude and your latitude. In other words, you know where you are, who you are, and where you are going and you can live your life based on your own self-excellence.

"Everything in life you do, you are not concentrating on self rather you are an escapist you don't want to concentrate on self, you don't want to face to self, you don't want to talk to self, you don't want to befriend yourself and you do everything else. Keep busy and then by habit you have no habit to relate to self and then you are exploited, then you are miserable, then you don't have self-esteem, you don't have self-respect, you don't know what you are, who you are, why you are."

There is a direct relationship between what you deliver and what you are; after all, they say "the proof is in the pudding". Self-determination is knowing what you're working with and what you have to work on. If you were a business person, you would have to know your income and outflow, and whether or not you were making a profit because to be in business, you have to be focused on making a profit. A successful business is the creative reflection of a self-determined businessperson who has the habit of self-analysis.

Successful artists concentrate on the self; they are self-determined, self-disciplined and practice self-analysis all the time. But they also concentrate on creative deliverance because a painting, a dance, a piece of music, a poem, a play or any other creative endeavor will ultimately lead to self-destruction if it is not released into the world. Every successful artist knows that it's their responsibility to share their work with the world and in order to do that, they must deliver at all costs.

PRANA, INSPIRATION AND THE RADIANT BODY

Prana is energy. Everything we do in Kundalini Yoga is to improve, increase and rejuvenate our energy. We teach that doing more things in our life that give us vitality will reduce the amount of stress we have. If we make better choices that add energy to our lives, rather than depleting it, we'll be healthier and happier as a result. It certainly is true for creative living; if you don't have enough prana, it will show up in your work, how you do or don't show up for people, how you handle situations, and the amount of stress you live with. A person who is short on prana, will have a problem with completion and deliverance. They will have doubts and fears. A person with a lot of prana tends to be positive and to follow through on things. They can handle many projects or jobs at once and know how to mange others to help them achieve their goals. A person with ample prana has energy to spare.

We get prana through the breath; the depth and consciousness of our breath is related to the amount of pranic energy we have and can hold. So, one of the first things any yogi learns is to become aware of the breath; how to breathe. I always tell the story of how my first two (pre-Kundalini) semi-private yoga lessons were just laying on the floor breathing. The teacher wouldn't even consider teaching yoga until we knew how to breathe.

Consider that the breath is directly connected to all your thoughts and emotions. Consider that mastering the breath promotes health and vitality, controls moods, develops concentration and contributes to a feeling of emotional security and connectedness. When you start becoming aware of the breath, you recognize that it works on the gross plane as a physical breath as well as on a subtle plane of the body/mind as prana.

Prana is not just the breath as you know it; it is the cosmic force that gives you life.

The reason why I teach and use Kundalini Yoga as a tool in my creative work is because it's a technology that works. What is the kundalini? It's your creative potential and it's an energy that all of us have at our disposal. When people ask me about the kundalini energy, I liken it to a financial inheritance. With a financial inheritance, you can invest it wisely, share it and use it for good. But used irresponsibly or badly invested, one can run through it quickly and end up with close to nothing in no time at all. In energetic terms, this would translate into stress, exhaustion, limitation, and creative immobility. Kundalini Yoga is a great tool for managing this "inheritance" so you never have to be without, you always have enough to share with others and with regard to creativity, you can always partake in it's limitless flow.

In the science of Kundalini Yoga, besides the chakras which most spiritually-minded people know something about, there are ten bodies: one physical, three mental, and six energetic. Most people at least acknowledge the physical body because they can see it, touch it, and experience it.

The mental bodies (negative, positive and neutral minds) process your thoughts, emotions and how you interact with your external world. The energetic bodies are just as real as the physical and mental bodies but we are not taught in this culture to relate to them. They are the soul body, the arc body, the auric body, the pranic body, the subtle body and the radiant body. There is also another energetic body, the eleventh, which is often thought of as the sound current; a pure state of consciousness that occurs when all the other bodies are in balance and under one's direction.

"The pranic body is out of place, there is no energy. If arc body is out of place, you have no defense mechanism. If mental negative is out of place, you cannot think about yourself. If mental positive is out of place, you cannot have the joy or bliss or ecstasy. If mental neutral is out of place, your every decision shall be wrong. If physical body out of place, whole thing will fall apart. If radiant body is out of place, you cannot convince anybody. If auric body is out of place, you are confused. If subtle body is out of place, the subtleties of life will be miles away from you. These are ten bodies; they all work, they are alive. When you will be dead your spiritual body will enter the subtle body and shall leave, you will loose about quarter ounce to an ounce of weight; that's the weight of two bodies."

For our purposes here, we'll be focusing on the pranic body (the breath) and the radiant body (the electromagnetic field). The pranic body is particularly important to creative types whose entire practice is hinged on nurturing an expansive perspective and limitless creative resources. The radiant body is important to creatives because it enables delivery.

There are 72,000 channels of energy in the body called *"nadis"*. You might know them by what they are called in Chinese medicine; the meridians. The flow of these channels make up the energy flow of the ten bodies; each of which has a specific form and function affecting us in important ways. If you knew how all these bodies affected your creative flow, you would never have to uninspired, unmotivated, stuck, or insecure ever again.

The life force is maintained and circulated by the pranic body. Our human machine is made to draw upon the cosmic pranic energy and that is what we live on. The study and practice of prana makes up a big part of yogic technology; how to get it, how to manage it, and how to use it. The physical body cannot live without it. Prana transforms the cells of the body and it transforms the mind. It can turn the tides by giving you the ability, energy, and power to alter your reality… remember, control your breath, control your mind. When you can control your mind, you can bring radical positivity and creativity to any situation.

When you breathe consciously, it gives you prosperity, it gives you projection and gives you personality. Why? Because it adds energy to your aura and you expand. Your expansion and fortification is directly related to the depth, rate and quality of your breath.

Think about this for a moment…we all talk about being "inspired" in order to be creative but have you ever considered what the world inspire means?

It actually has two meanings: 1) to fill (someone) with the urge or ability to do or feel something, especially to do something creative; *and* 2) to breathe in (air); inhale.

Naturally, it stands to reason that in order to be "inspired", one has to consciously breathe. Prana therefore has a profound effect on Creative Living. Expansion of the lungs and ribcage allows for more prana to be inhaled and thus, the mind expands. When the mind expands, so does your limitless creative potential. And, to top it off, all this prana gives you energy; the kind of energy that Yogi Bhajan called the "keep up spirit".

The keep up spirit is your radiant body; it will give you the courage and self-confidence you need to exceed your own expectations, to become fully and wholly creative, astonishingly resourceful, and completely and totally limitless. I mean, can you imagine having a life of limitless potential? Working on the radiant body will give you that and more.

Your radiance makes you literally shine in any circumstance and gives you the power to takes things all the way to the finish line. When you talk about creative living you HAVE to acknowledge the importance and power of the radiant body because without it, you simply cannot brings things to completion. You simply cannot deliver. And what do you suppose is the most direct way to build the radiant body?

That's right…through the breath!

"What is Pranayam? Purifying the blood and circulating the oxygen; purifying the circulatory system. Prana is the single most important element in the body. What is Prana? Prana is what comes in your life through the breath. We call it breath of life."

There is a wide range of pranayama available in Kundalini Yoga, which one can use to manage different states of consciousness, employ relaxation, and initiate states of well-being conducive to creativity. Simple breath exercises and techniques can be extremely useful in getting projects from conception to deliverance, by helping to overcome fear, quiet the ego, and giving you the strength and the willingness to let go.

An important thing I want to add - Sometimes when we have to deliver something …which can be speaking in public, releasing a book, attending your own art opening, performing on a stage, or just plain "putting it out there", we get butterflies in our stomach or cold feet or what is called performance anxiety. That nervousness and excitement is a gift. It is pure energy, pure prana that is given to you to use in your endeavor. When you shift your mindset from performance   anxiety to performance enhancer, you will be surprised how pleasurable that "nervous" feeling can become.

WILLINGNESS AND THE STRENGTH TO LET GO

"You can conceive, you can remain pregnant but you cannot remain pregnant indefinitely. Delivery doesn't take place, you can die. You should have ego, let it go also. You have a thought, let it go. To go, lies in let it go. The secret of going and reaching and enjoying the destination, reaching the destination, the destiny, lies in letting it happen. You can start the engine, you can put the gear, you can give the gas, but if you don't let the brake go, car cannot move. Without brakes driving car is dangerous, I agree. But not with full-applied brakes you think it is going to go? No, it is not going to go. It is going to sit there. Finally your gas will be out or you gear will be out. Something has to go out if the brake won't let it go."

A person who is new to making art, will often find it difficult to give an art piece away; it feels like you are giving away a part of yourself. I remember in the young artist me, the reluctance to part with a painting or drawing - there is most definitely a tension; a resistance to letting go of it. The more you do this, however, the better you get at it. Even though most artists have been practicing this "letting go" business for a long time, there are still some instances where it feels exactly like the first time and putting your work out into the public realm can seem like an impossible task. In the case of the performative arts, it might manifest as stage fright or performance anxiety.

Letting go is an art in itself. In most religions and spiritual practices, letting go is considered to be the foundation of happiness. Attachment to negative emotions, bad habits, and toxic relationships is as common as being attached to beautiful things and pleasurable moments. But no matter how hard we try, we manage somehow to get attached to the most peculiar and inexplicable things…

There is a hedge that is planted outside my bedroom window of the apartment that I rent. It's a ubiquitous plant, *Ligustrum japonicum 'Texanum'* otherwise known as Japanese or Wax-leaf Privet; planted in gardens all over Southern California. In it's natural state, it is a fluffy and spreading dense green small tree that can grow up to 10 feet tall and about 6-8 feet wide. The flowering period, when it's leaves are tipped with bunches of tiny sweet smelling white flowers, is the best part of the privet life cycle. In competition with star jasmine and some of the other heavy scented spring flowering hedges, the privet in blossom is an absolute joy; it smells sweet in a gentle and refined kind of way.

One of my pleasures is enjoying the smell of the blossoms as it wafts into the open windows of my apartment, however this is a pleasure I cannot allow myself to become attached to. Several times a year, when I least expect it, the gardeners cut the blossoms as they shape the privets into flowerless lollypops. And each time it happens, I get better and better at letting my attachment to it go. It is, like most things in life, a fleeting pleasure that I cannot and never will possess.

"We abide nowhere, we possess nothing."

~ Chatral Rinpoche ~

Most things in life are like that yet we still aim to claim it all for ourselves. Attachment leads to self-induced human suffering and it is completely avoidable. In the case of creativity, non-deliverance or holding back one's work goes against the natural law. To consider NOT delivering an artwork or project can be due to many factors: lack of energy, lack of willpower, lack of self-determination, overpowering fear, unhealthy attachment, and laziness.

"When you begin your work of art, a certain drive develops and that drive should be absent of laziness. You might have a great theme that you want to execute, so you have to go on constantly in accord with your vision of what you want to do. If you cut down your full vision, and create a work of art at half-vision level, that is breaking the discipline or morality of artistic endeavor. So there has to be an absence of laziness. In other words, when we want to produce a work of art, we should do it all the way." - Chögyam Trungpa

Doing it "all the way" takes the willingness and strength to let go of our attachments to outcome, worldly goods, acceptance from outside sources, self-destructive habits or life's sweet pleasures. You cannot overcome temptations (maya) if you are lazy in your efforts. When you are working on any deliverable project, you have be diligent, you have to be self-disciplined, and as you probably could have guessed by now, be willing to tackle the ego because **all attachments come from the ego.**

For example, think about all the energy you waste on worrying about what other people think of you or what you do. If you cultivated your infinite intuition instead of your limited ego-insecurity, your life would become so very vast, unlimited, and free. If you'd strengthen your intuition, you'd know that most everything, good or bad is neither possess-able nor permanent. If you use intuition as your guidance system, Yogi Bhajan said that you will always be supported by the Universe. When you start to live life from your intuition instead of your ego, you automatically begin to let go.

"The Shashara, the thousand-petal lotus, the intellect gives you thousand thoughts per wink of the eye. Out of million thoughts some become feelings, some become desires, some become emotions, and something becomes attachment and that is drag. When you tie a dog you think that is happy? Then you put a bird in the cage, that's happy? Similarly when you attach yourself how can you be happy? Your nature is Infinite and you live confined. There is something to learn. If you learn intuition you will be happy."

ART OF DELIVERANCE HIGHLIGHTS

1. What you deliver is who you are

2. You must learn the technology of how to pull yourself out of your animal nature and discard your attachment to the ego.

3. If you don't deliver, you will destroy yourself… that's just how it works. Deliverance and destruction are two sides of the same coin.

4. If you want to be successful in whatever you do, then you have to ask yourself just how visible, vocal, accessible and active do you want to be? Your success is directly related to the answers to these questions.

5. The Art of Deliverance requires 1) willpower, 2) self- determination 3) prana and radiance and 4) the strength and willingness to let go.

6. Every successful artist knows that it's their responsibility to share their work with the world and in order to do that, they must deliver at all costs.

7. When working on any deliverable, you must be determined to crush the ego because all attachments come from the ego.

8. "Letting go gives us freedom, and freedom is the only condition for happiness. If, in our heart, we still cling to anything – anger, anxiety, or possessions – we cannot be free." - Thich Nat Hanh

9. I you have stage fright, think of that nervousness and excitement as a gift from the Universe. It is your pure excitement, pure energy, pure *prana that is given to you to use in your endeavor. Breathe!Suggest*

SAT KRIYA

...IMPROVES general physical heath because all the internal organs Receive a gentle rhythmic massage

... Strengthens the HEART Because of THE RHYTHMIC UP AND-DOWN OF BLOOD PRESSURE generated from the pumping of the NAvel point.

... OPENS UP THE CREATIVE FLOW AND gets RID OF FEAR.

...IS FUNDAMENTAL TO KUNDALINI YOGA and should be practiced every day for at least 3 minutes. ITS EFFECTS are numerous

... WORKS DIRECTLY ON STIMULATING AND CHAN-NELIZING THE KUNDALINI ENERGY SO IT MUST BE PRACTICED WITH THE MANTRA SAT NAM.

... BENEFITS THOSE WHO ARE SEVERELY mal-adjusted OR have mental problems because these disturbances are always connected to an imbalance in the energies of the lower 3 chakras.

HOW TO DO SAT KRIYA:

SIT ON The heels with the arms overhead and palms together. Interlace the fingers except for the index fingers, which point straight up. MEN, cross the right thumb over the left thumb; women cross the left thumb over the right. Chant SAT and pull the navel point IN AND UP, chant NAM and relax it.

Continue for at least 3 minutes (or whatever time is specified in the kriya you're doing) TO END: INHALE, apply Root Lock (mulbandh) and squeeze the muscles tightly from the buttocks all the way up the back, past the shoulders. Mentally allow the energy to flow through the top of the skull. EXHALE, hold the breath out and apply all the locks (mahabandh). INHALE..... and relax.

NOTE: whenever Sat Kriya is done in a Kundalini Yoga kriya, the rule of thumb is to apply root lock on the inhale and maha-bandh on the exhale, even though it may not be specified.

✱ YOU MAY BUILD THE TIME OF SAT KRIYA TO 31 MINUTES, BUT remember to HAVE A Long deep relaxation immediately after.

SAT KRIYA CONTINUED

✳ A good way to BUILD up the time is to do the KRIYA for 3 minutes, then rest 2 minutes. Repeat this cycle until you have completed 15 MINUTES OF SAT KRIYA AND 10 MINUTES OF REST. FINISH the required relaxation by resting an additional 15-20 MINUTES. DO NOT TRY TO JUMP to 31 MINUTES Because you feel you are strong, virile or happen to be a yoga teacher. RESPECT THE INHERENT POWER OF THE TECHNIQUE. Let the kriya prepare the ground of your Body properly TO PLANT the seed of Higher experience. IT IS NOT JUST AN EXERCISE, IT IS A KRIYA THAT WORKS ON ALL LEVELS OF YOUR BEING..... KNOWN AND UNKNOWN. You might block the more subtle experiences of higher energies by pushing the physical Body too much. You could have a HUGE rush of energy. You may have an experience of higher consciousness, but NOT be able to integrate the experience into your psyche. So... prepare yourself with constancy, patience & moderation. THE END RESULT IS ASSURED.

✳ IF you have not taken drugs or have cleared your system of all their effects, you may choose to practice this KRIYA with the palms OPEN, pressing flat against each other. this releases more energy than the other method. It is generally NOT taught this way in a public class because maybe someone may have weak nerves from drug use.

✳ NOTICE that you emphasize pulling the NAVEL point IN (ON "SAT) Don't try to apply mulbandh. Mulbandh (root lock) happens automatically and naturally AS the NAVEL is pulled. THE HIPS and the Lumbar spine do NOT rotate or FLEX and the arms do not jerk back and forward. Your spine stays straight and the ONLY motion your arms make is A slight UP + DOWN stretch with your chest lifting with each Sat Nam.

✳ Sat KRIYA strengthens the entire sexual system and stimulate its natural FLOW of energy. THIS relaxes phobias about sexuality. It allows you to control the insistent sexual impulse by rechannelizing sexual energy to CREATIVE AND HEALING activities IN THE BODY.

ART OF IMPACT

CREATING ELEVATED VIBRATIONS

Yogi Bhajan said that *"creativity is nothing else but to create impact"* and of all the chapters in this book, I get the most excited by the potential of this idea.

The dictionary definition of impact is the force of impression of one thing on another. As an artist, I know that anything I create will have some sort of impact on the viewer or audience. Even in my day to day life, I know that my words and actions can be just as impactful as an object or performance I create. Who I am and what I deliver determines my impact and this can have a transformative effect on others whether I intend it to or not. That is why it's so important to understand that everything you deliver has its consequences, good or bad and therefore you can create either a positive or negative impact on others.

If you can create an elevated positive impact on others, then that is the best use of living to your creative potential.

"Impact is your highest virtue. It's not impression, it's not winning, it is not losing, it is not convincing, it is not conquering, nothing of all that sort which you know means a thing. It is your personality impact which becomes your reality in your own life. And it owns you. You understand that? When you discontinue the inflow and you disturb the impact, you create the

ripples, you create the tears, you create the cracks and you devalue the value of your own personality."

Making art, making friends, making business associates, making a name for yourself...it is all according to the impact you have. Call it a first impression or a lasting effect, impact has nothing to do with wealth or poverty, happiness or unhappiness. Impact is what effect your actions have on others or on your community. Period.

Impact is the initial imprint which you create. When you are in a state of flourishing, you are nurturing the creative act, the project, what ever you are preparing for delivery; the impact of which is the result of all that you do, all that you are. Your life depends on your deliverance: "What you deliver, that is what you are"...and that, my friends, depends entirely on the impact that you have.

INFLOW AND IMPACT

Inflow and outflow of creativity should always be in balance. Think of breathing; the inhale feeds the exhale, exhale feeds the inhale. Inflow is the by-product of uplinking to the Creative Cosmic Flow channel. Inflow is when the thought waves become ideas. Inflow is what feeds your personal ecosystem which consists of your spiritual practice, your promoting habits, your patterns, your responsibilities, your commitments, your environment, etc. All these things feed your creativity and it is a continuous orbit of energies that you are trying to nurture by putting the inflow and outflow in balance.

"Life is held by impact and it is fed by inflow". You have to feed your creativity and you do it with inflow.

Let's say you are making a project. Given the circumstances, the parameters of the project, your responsibility, and your artistic practice and acumen, it must be in balance with the outcome. You must be able to handle the impact it may or may not have. What is it's social, political, historical implications? Will it offend? Will it please? Will it uplift? Will it make people angry? Are you fit to handle the outcome? If creativity is nothing else but to create impact, you have to make sure your body, mind, spirit are up to the task! Fearlessness, risk-taking, nervous system bandwidth, compassion, power over your mind and emotions are all strengths you can develop with your yoga practice.

"Your impact is your trust under which you survive, live and advance. And your inflow if is harmonious it's your strength, it's your attraction, it will bring you opportunities, but if you cause crack ripples and that kind of stuff you are going to blow it."

You could say that your impact has almost everything to do with your aura. The auric body is one of the six energetic bodies I wrote about in the last chapter. People who have a very strong aura or electromagnetic field have a very strong life force and they can, with just a touch and/or mental projection, liberate others, uplift them, make a lasting impression. When a person has a very strong auric body, they are neither negative to themselves nor to another person. In other words, they can have a powerful positive impact on others.

Without impact you don't exist; nobody knows you were there. As a creative person, you know how important it is for both you and your work to make an impression. Your aura and how you feed it and keep it strong will do that for you; that is your inflow.

Yogi Bhajan talked about how important it was to create a inflow that was consistent and harmonious. This might be thought of as your daily practice, your self-discipline, how you show up for yourself and for others. *He also said it was crucial not to hide one's "handicaps" but to instead of covering up, admit to mistakes and failings and to work towards improvement and correction.*

"Understand what ... your inflow is. And you can have it as you want it. Never disturb the inflow, make it better. Make it clear, make it permanent, make it rhythmic, create harmony and interlock the impact and let the flow create the interflow. You understand what I am saying? Start today, forget tomorrow, drop yesterday. Don't live in this guilt and past, it's very difficult to get out of it. Do you understand what I am saying? Yesterday is yesterday, it's gone. Today you learnt inflow and impact ... pick it up, start working. Just be aware of it. It will be all done. The worst thing in inflow we do is, we cover our handicaps."

Assessing your inflow is part of the self-determination, so essential for the Art of Delivery that I wrote about in the last chapter. If you are feeling irritated or frustrated or out of sorts, just look at where you are; what's coming in and what's going out. Are all the channels that are coming in, your inflow, working okay? Are you making the kind of impact you want to have?

Most of the time you can put things in balance by self-examination and strengthening your aura.

AURA AND IMPACT

"Those people who are humble, affectionate, serving, and who breathe the Divine Force into themselves, make their mind concentrate on the breath, and prayto the Universal Spirit by tuning in—not only does their own magnetic field/electric power get charged because of the life force, their circumvent force becomes so strong that it can keep away all the negative forces, and they can change the destiny of others."

Creativity runs on energy and everyone's auric field is vibrating with that energy. When you are in your full creative power, it shows up in your aura. The aura surrounds the body of all things and in humans, it has the potential to expand to nine feet in all directions. Wearing white natural fiber clothing is just one very simple way you can strengthen and extend your aura. A strong aura will attract opportunities and help you to make positive choices. Like a shield of protection, it will repel all forms of negativity; psychic, infectious, and emotional. It will give you a strong sense of identity, personal strength, and self-confidence. A weak aura will do the opposite; making you insecure and vulnerable, letting negativity penetrate your mind and body.

When you walk into a room, it is the aura that announces your arrival. It tells everyone who you are and what you are about. It is the aura that makes the first impression and the impact.

When you start to understand how it all works, you can use your energy to turn the cards in your favor. You can be seen when you want to be seen, and you can disappear when you need to retreat. You can create projects, situations, relationships that will be remembered; affect the socio-political landscape, have tremendous impact on your community, and make people feel better.

"It is very creative to be angry, it is absolutely creative to be depressed, and wonderfully creative and objectively to be neurotic, yeah, it is creative, believe me or not. And there is nothing more creative but to be obnoxious and supreme quality of creativity is to be corrupt and dishonest, and disloyal. This is all creative, because it needs energy to create a atmosphere in which you can project and create a atmosphere of impact."

Remember that it is the same creative energy to be noble, to be pure, to be loyal and trustworthy, to make good on your commitments, to create new ideas and products, solve problems, and as Yogi Bhajan said *"discover new elements in the universe or in the society, help and counsel constantly on the positive notes, socialize, smile, uplift, elevate fellow human beings."*

What is YOUR gift? Imagine if you could use your talents for something that could help humanity, the planet and possibly heal community. I'm not saying that artists shouldn't make work for themselves…explore their own divine nature and all that… but you might consider working on projects that deal with larger issues like social justice and raising the vibration of the planet. It all starts with you, however. When you start to improve your self instead of trying to fix the people around you, you make the kind of changes that other people feel and are deeply impacted by. Make other people feel better about themselves and you are doing God's work. People need to be heard; they want to be understood. Being aware of how you impact others will give you a whole new perspective on what you can use your creativity for.

Maybe you don't think you have a gift....I will most likely disagree with you, but if you still don't think that you do, then think of your job. How can you infuse your job with creative energy so that you can make the people you interact with feel good? Think of your family. How can you bring creativity to your home life, to the way you interact so that family members feel heard and supported? If you are having a good time, everyone you come in contact with will have a good time, too. Listening to yourself will teach you how to listen to others. Getting rid of your own neurosis will help others to get rid of theirs. **Your positivity will be positively infectious!**

CREATIVE IMPACT AND GOOD VIBRATIONS

I want to give you a few examples of how all this works. Impact can be a very subtle thing and yet be a very powerful thing at the same time. Your life or your creative project is completely under your control and you can orchestrate how you or your projects are perceived and received. In some cases the outcome can be random, but I'll discuss that in a bit.

"Synchronize your own magnetic field with the cosmic magnetic field which has a complete interconnection with all other humans, other existences, and realms of material existence."

Investigating the "space between", in particular the liminal or interstitial quality of time and space is the primary subject of Hirokazu Kosaka's art practice. He combines his site-specific large-scale sculptural installations with music, Kyudo archery, performance, calligraphy, visual art practice and dance; a synthesis of disciplines that opens up new ways of being, seeing, and listening. Although he grew up in an 800-year old Buddhist monastery and was raised as a monk, Kosaka was trained in Shingon Buddhism, a much older and more esoteric denomination than Zen. It was there he learned the ancient creative and meditative disciplines of calligraphy and Japanese archery, both of which he still practices today. In his archery practice, Kosaka speaks about the notion of the "perfect shot"; the archer, the bow and arrow and the target all become one. With regard to creative impact, it is his archery practice and performances I'd like to tell you about.

When one studies Kyudo archery, it involves the meditative discipline of reading Buddhist sutras for breath control. A year can go by before a student is permitted to shoot an arrow. It takes a long time to master the basic lessons in breathing, walking, sitting, and the placement of weight. Hitting a 1/16 of an inch piece of straw is the ultimate goal; the impact being the culmination of all that intense training and practice.

There are no bull's eyes or targets, just the round bale of hay on a stand. Discussing Kyudo, Kosaka mentions *"a performance tradition that goes back hundreds of years"* in Buddhist monasteries. *"I think how I walk on a stage and how I am focused on a stage, anything I do, is aiming for that 1/16 of an inch of straw,"* he says.

To behold a Kyudo performance is to understand what inflow and impact is all about. Kosaka explains, *"It becomes a search for one's path, for one's spirit. . . . I think when I face the straw, the hole in the straw, I'm trying to kill myself, meaning 'I, the ego.' I want to shoot that, and it's really difficult. . . ."*

In your life, in my life…we are just preparing ourselves to gracefully shoot arrows into the banishment of ego and, at the same time, to leave a lasting impression. When we make art or are being creative in our lives, we are vibrating at a particular frequency and those who are vibrating at that same frequency will "get" the art (or the action) and the impact it was intended to have. Strengthening the aura, conscious breathing, deep listening, neutral attention, moving the body, repeating mantra, meditation, just paying close attention to the details of day to day life, uplinking, conceiving, delivering …these are all contributors to your vibrational frequency.

When you talk about the law of vibration, you might as well be talking about the law of life. They are basically the same thing; if you are not vibrating, you are not living, case in point. The universe and everything in it is vibrating all the time. Our cells vibrate; atoms, electrons, protons, neutrons … they all vibrate. When I talk, i am vibrating. If you are listening to me, you are vibrating, too. If when I talk and you listen, we are not in tune with each other at the same frequency, you won't understand a word I am saying. That's why you must resonate at the vibratory frequency of truth - it casts the widest and most elevated net.

"My strength lies I do not intellectualize anything, I do not justify things. I strike at a very wide beautiful target, that is heart. Man can do all tricks but he is very much weak before his own heart. And if you tune in into somebody and tune in into his consciousness and you focus at his heart and on his third eye, he cannot answer you. He'll go dumb right there and then. Because truth is the base of everybody. And if you face a person with **truth,** you will straightaway understand what life is."

Throughout his life Allan Kaprow, who called himself an "un-artist", created work outside of traditional art venues. His performance-based spontaneous group interactions, called Happenings, were scripted collages of movement, sound, smells and light and what put him in the forefront of the art world of the 1950s and 1960s.

For Kaprow, the modernist practice of art was much more than the production of objects; it involved the disciplined effort to engage, observe and interpret the processes of living that he felt were as important as the "art" itself; in other words, Kaprow used experience as the medium of his art practice. When Kaprow writes in his essay Nontheatrical Performance (1976) about paying attention to ones ordinary life, he is describing the core of his practice: **the art of conscious being.** This is the backbone of each and every spiritual practice and takes the form of an ongoing inquiry or research that all artists and spiritual practitioners share. He writes:

"When you view a normal routine in your life as a performance and carefully chart for a month how you greet someone each day, what you say with your body, your pauses, and your clothing; and when you carefully chart the responses you get – this can be basic research."

Kaprow describes the un-artist as someone who started out as a conventional artist and at some point has an epiphany about the value of making art that reminds them of the rest of their lives. Kaprow, a Zen Buddhist embodies his spiritual practice in his "non-art" practice. I believe that the core of this book is centered on the idea that we are all creative, we are all artists and that the epiphany Kaprow describes, illuminates in both directions. *I propose that an artist can be someone who starts out as a "conventional person" and at some point along the way has an epiphany about the creative potential of their lives.*

Some of us identify as artists from the get-go; there was never any choice in the matter for me. But there are so many individuals who don't think they are creatives or artists and buy into the myth that being an artist is about being able to perform certain culturally accepted skills like drawing realistically, or playing recognizable music or dancing on a stage in a ballet …all of which require a certain degree of "recognized" success.

Art does exist in the everyday performance of tasks, which is Kaprow's whole point. Cooking for friends, making a comfortable home, tending a garden and even making art out of un-arty actions like organizing or cleaning can have tremendous impact.

While other artists doing "lifelike art" (what Kaprow referred to as what he was doing) used larger public formats for the staging of events, he opted for smaller, more intimate personal projects that he called activities. It was these activities that were the manifestation of his longtime Zen practice and in which he found the affinity between a meditation practice and just being and doing.

Kaprow wrote in Art Form in 1990:

"What happens when you pay close attention to anything, especially routine behavior, is that it changes. Attention alters what is attended. So lifelike art plays somewhere in and

between attention to physical process and attention to interpretation. It is experience, yet it is ungraspable. It requires quotation marks ('lifelike') but sheds them as the un-artist sheds art."

These activity projects were accompanied by books that were conceived of in the style of neutralized, depersonalized instruction manuals and Kaprow produced a large body of them; meant to be interpreted and acted out by participants… who could be anybody.

These project books serve as a link between the artist, their audience, the participants, and the work itself. Although not considered conventional art, Kaprow and others like him, created a positive impact on society and the art world by testing social convention, boundaries and art world definitions. And, of course, by calling attention to the creative value in mundane daily activities, introduced the art world to a profound and timeless spiritual practice.

DHARMA ART AND CREATIVE LIVING

Kaprow's art practice is in alignment in many ways to the Buddhist idea of Dharma Art. In his beautiful book, True Perception; the Path of Dharma Art, Chögyam Trungpa begins the chapter on Art in Everyday Life with:

"Awareness practice is not just sitting meditation or meditation-in-action alone. It is a unique training practice in how to behave as an inspired human being. That is what is meant by being an artist."

In Dharma Art or another name for it, "genuine meditation art", you would not be worried or fearful about what other people think of your work. You don't judge it and it's therefore impossible to fail at it. So therefore, you end up making something for the pure pleasure of making it and so "getting blocked" simply is NOT an issue.

With these conditions, a "masterpiece" could come out of an untrained person if they were in the right state of mind… although it probably would not be a predictable outcome. As with all other facets of life, one *might require a teacher or mentor to pass down skills, knowledge, and the tricks of the trade and with practice, mastery would be possible. A layman or untrained person does, however possess a certain point of view that is enviable at times:*

"I do not agree that that layman's opinion is less of a valid judgement of music than that of a professional musician. In fact, I would often rely more on the judgement of a sensitive layman than that of a professional since the professional, because of his constant involvement with the mechanics of music, must fight to preserve the naiveté that the layman already possesses." - Bill Evans

The key ingredient in Dharma Art is that the artist possesses a sense of ease and total self-confidence. So much art in this modern world is produced under pressure with worry and fear so this concept of creative ease might be new to some. We are so wrapped up in what other people think about us and our work, that our creative life ends up being based on impressing or taking advantage of others, gaining recognition or fame, making money or beating out the competition. When we make art for these purposes, it is an aggressive act and it is robbing us of the pleasure of self-discovery.

That is why Dharma Art is sometimes described as a non-aggressive creative activity. And when you are practicing Dharma art, you are not only engaged in the act of self-discovery, you are practicing Creative Living. Just like with Kaprow's "life-like art", appreciating things as they are is important when discussing Dharma Art. "Discovering the elegance in everyday life" is another way of putting it. It has nothing to do with the production of art or being the first to have a cool idea. It has absolutely nothing to do with ego. It's about one's state of mind; that's the first and most important thing about it.

The second thing is to consider is figuring out how can you organize your life so that you can afford to create beauty..but not at the expense or the suffering of others. In Dharma Art, one is paying attention to the basic reality of life; how things are arranged and prepared, appreciating the work that goes into making something, how things sound, taste, smell rather than just filling galleries with paintings. It's about learning how to live; how to eat, how to clean, how to work with your basic reality. It's not only learning how to take care of your tools, its learning how to take care of your mind.

"An **artist takes great care of his tools, his brushes, his pens --he selects his material, his wood, clay, paper, etc. with close consideration as to what will provide the most responsive medium for his talents. Yet the fundamental tool, the mind is left wandering, undisciplined and full of conflicting desires. The mind is largely an unknown factor in the process of creation. It is necessary to be able to tune the mind to the basic life forces within and**

without and to be able to relax the mental processes so that the spontaneous creative impulses can come through clearly and honestly."

A person who is living creatively is full of appreciation for all of these thing as well as being non-competitive, non-aggressive, intuitive, self-confident and content. In both Buddhist and Yogic practices, if your mind is preoccupied with aggression, you absolutely cannot function properly, however, Trungpa believed that if your mind was preoccupied with passion, you might have a chance.

Think about what passion is for a second…it's a heightened interest in the quality of something that makes you want to explore every little thing about it. This focus and concentration makes you forget your aggression for a while and it ends up being a pure, positive endeavor. When you are in the flourishing stage of creativity, you are an altered state of passionate focus which is both intoxicating and fulfilling. The creative energy is flowing, you are beyond time and space, all the ego-driven neurosis - the self-doubt, the competitiveness, the aggressiveness vanish in the presence of one-pointed passion.

Trungpa writes that you can neither learn Dharma Art nor teach it; you discover it by setting up an environment in which it can be discovered. It seems then that Dharma Art exists in a state of pure consciousness where you are nothing but a vessel for the flow of pure gratitude and joy. In Kundalini yoga, there is a state in which you become nothing; it is said that in this state, all powers will prevail through you. It's called shuniya (or shunia) and when you experience or discover it, you can easily access your soul without all those noisy neurotic distractions.

"I think that, in a sense, performing is the closest you can get to a spiritual discipline and I think of it very much as a spiritual discipline because I'm always working on focusing and keeping open at the same time and I'm always working on opening the doors of my heart so that my heart is reaching the heart of those people in the audience and somehow bypassing discursive thought, bypassing that judge that's always in there".
- Meredith Monk, artist and musician

When you are making art and you are interested in it and passionate about it, you feel like you are on a hero's quest and are thrilled and excited with the process. If you are not passionate about what you are doing, you will feel stuck and find a million reasons to be distracted. Passion in combination with discipline produces terrific results! When passion is undisciplined…well, as we all know, that's another story.

If The Art of Creating Impact is to create elevated vibrations, then to cultivate an attitude of non-aggressiveness would be the ideal way to go. Flowing through you, the creative force can take shape as a thing…a product…a project or it can engender self-discovery and the appreciation of daily actions and encounters.

ART OF IMPACT HIGHLIGHTS

1. Yogi Bhajan said that "creativity is nothing else but to create impact".

2. If you can create an elevated positive impact on others, then that is the best use of living to your creative potential.

3. Inflow and outflow of creativity should always be in balance. You have to feed your creativity and you do it with inflow.

4. Your impact is related to the strength of your your aura. With just a touch and/or mental projection, you can liberate, uplift, and have a powerful positive impact on others.

5. What is YOUR gift? Imagine if you could use your gift for something that could help humanity. Imagine looking beyond your own self-expression and seeing how your gift could make other people happy.

6. Strengthening the aura which includes conscious breathing, deep listening, neutral attention, moving the body, repeating mantra, meditation, just paying close attention to the details of day to day life; these are all contributors to your vibrational frequency; your inflow as it were. And when you start paying attention, your aura changes. It creates potential.

7. I propose that an artist can be someone who starts out as a conventional person and at some point has an epiphany about the creative potential of their lives

FOR CREATIVITY

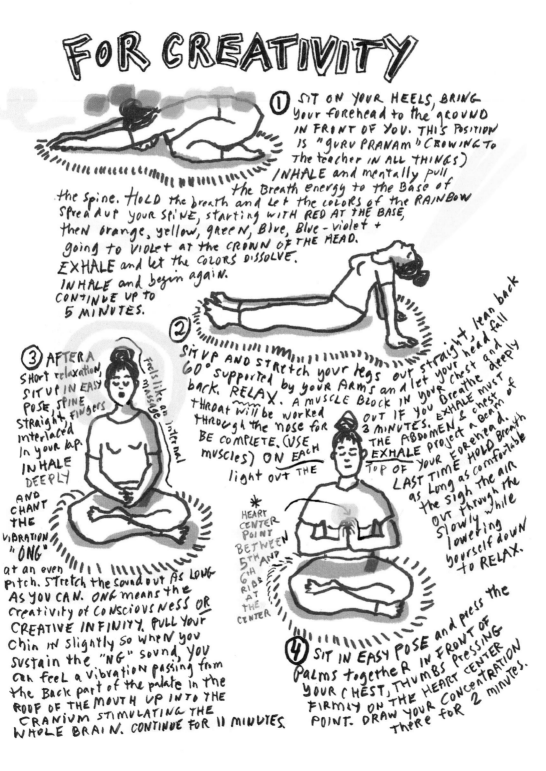

① SIT ON YOUR HEELS, BRING Your forehead to the GROUND IN FRONT OF YOU. THIS POSITION IS "GURU PRANAM" (BOWING TO The teacher IN ALL THINGS) INHALE and mentally pull the Breath energy to the Base of the spine. HOLD the breath and Let the coLors of the RAINBOW Spread up your SPINE, starting WITH RED AT THE BASE, then orange, yellow, green, Blue, Blue-violet + going to VIOLET at the CROWN OF THE HEAD. EXHALE and let the COLORS DISSOLVE. INHALE and begin again. CONTINUE UP TO 5 MINUTES.

② SIT UP AND STRETCH your legs out straight, lean back 60° supported by your ARMS and let your head fall back. RELAX. A MUSCLE BLOCK IN your chest and throat will be worked OUT IF you Breathe deeply through the nose for 3 MINUTES. EXHALE must BE COMPLETE. (USE THE ABDOMEN & chest of muscles) ON EACH EXHALE project a Beam of light out THE TOP OF YOUR FOREHEAD. LAST TIME HOLD Breath as Long as comfortable then SIGH the air OUT through the mouth while slowly lowering yourself down to RELAX.

③ AFTER A short relaxation, SIT UP IN EASY POSE, SPINE straight, fingers interlaced In your lap. INHALE DEEPLY AND CHANT THE VIBRATION "ONG" at an even pitch. Stretch the sound out AS LONG AS YOU CAN. ONG means the creativity of CONSCIOUSNESS OR CREATIVE INFINITY. PULL YOUR chin IN slightly so when you sustain the "NG" sound, you can feel a vibration passing from the Back part of the palate in the ROOF OF THE MOUTH UP INTO THE CRANIUM stimulating THE WHOLE BRAIN. CONTINUE FOR 11 MINUTES.

Feels like an internal massage

* HEART CENTER POINT BETWEEN 5TH AND 6TH RIBS AT THE CENTER

④ SIT IN EASY POSE and press the palms together IN FRONT OF YOUR CHEST, THUMBS PRESSING FIRMLY ON THE HEART CENTER POINT. DRAW YOUR CONCENTRATION There for 2 minutes.

⑤ Begin Rubbing your palms Together vigorously, creating heat between them. Rub them for 2 minutes, sensing the energy building up in your palms. Then draw the palms 4 inches apart, facing each other and feel the POLARITY of attraction and repulsion; Right palm positive, left palm negative. CLOSE YOUR EYES and feel the sensitivity in your palms for 2 minutes.

⑥ SHIFT THE HANDS so that the right hand is cupped facing down and left hand is cupped, facing up. They should be 4 inches apart, the heart center lying midway between them.
Begin Breathing DEEP and Relaxed through the Nostrils, gathering the breath energy between the palms, sensing it there as a glowing ball of Light. Do this for 4 minutes.

Relay into it

smile a bit.... you are OPENING YOUR HEART. The interplay of the electromagnetic forces of the body in this meditation will act to Relax those tissues in the chest and chest cavity

⑦ PRESS YOUR RIGHT PALM FIRMLY against the heart center and bring your left arm behind your back so the back of the left hand is pressed on the spine OPPOSITE the right palm. Feel the charging polarity thus set up, and begin BREATH OF FIRE, breathin' rapidly and vigorously through the NOSTRILS.... USING the NAVEL POINT AS A PUMP. AFTER 2 MINUTES, INHALE DEEPLY and hold as long as is comfortable and EXHALE. Meditate quietly for a few minutes with your spine straight and your hands in your lap, FEELING DIVINE. ♡ ♡ ♡

"Highly creative is, live
as a character actor,
most beautiful gift is,
give somebody elevated
vibrations. Soothe people,
get rid of your negativity and your
corruption, so that people can start
liking you and following you, create a
image of grace…give people hope."

Yogi Bhajan

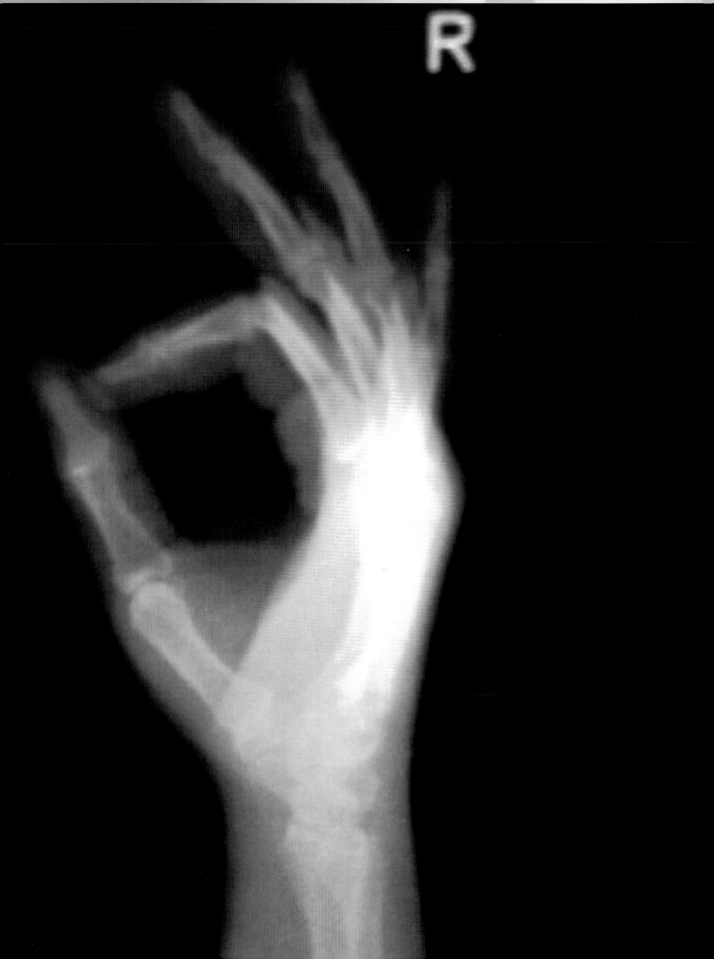

ART OF HEALING

"The art of healing, the art of ecstasy, the art of God-consciousness has millions of names in mystic terms. It has to do with rhythm and reality. When the body is in rhythm, there is ease. When the body, or any part of the body goes out of rhythm, there is dis-ease."

FINDING YOUR RHYTHM

Healing is the process of returning to balance. It is neither a cure nor an end result. The word "cure" implies that there is no more work to be done, but there is always work to be done. Your blood chemistry, your psyche, and every cell of your body changes within a seventy-two hour period. Healing is process-based continuous action; the magnetic frequency of your cells are in constant motion. Much like creativity, love, and prosperity, healing energy can be generated and irrigated into a flow.

You could say that we are always in a state of healing except for when the flow gets interrupted or you get out of rhythm. In fact, when you are in the divine creative flow, or experiencing expansive unconditional love or feeling your cup runneth over, you are more likely to experience self-healing and develop the gift for healing others. It's all interrelated.

Healing is an art. Healing is another name for being "in the flow". The reason it's considered one of the Eleven Yogic Arts is because it requires the same awareness and connectivity to divine source as all the yogic arts I'm writing about in this book. Both creativity and healing are pure expressions of your soul; they need to cultivated to that they can shared or delivered. And finally, the impact of healing is that your body, mind and soul become in sync with the rhythm of the cosmos and everything just gets better.

"Music creates order out of chaos: for rhythm imposes unanimity upon the divergent, melody imposes continuity upon the disjointed, and harmony imposes compatibility upon the incongruous" - Yehudi Menuhin, violinist and conductor

On a purely physical level, we can get sick if we do not process and metabolize the food we eat, but we can also get sick if we do not process and metabolize our emotions. Because the body and the mind are deeply interconnected, oftentimes the body will alert you to deeper emotional or psychic issues that need to be addressed.

For example, you might experience mid to lower back pain that you would normally attribute to lifting something heavy or pulling a muscle. But consider that, because the kidneys hold fear energy, the pain might have something to do with not processing that feeling. I've experienced many occasions where just by turning my attention to how I might not be dealing with an emotion effectively (i.e; fear or worry) has caused the symptoms to disappear. You might find that when you have a sore throat, it might have something to do with not saying something that needs to be said. the unexpressed can literally get stuck in your throat!

"Where I come from we say that rhythm is the soul of life, because the whole universe revolves around rhythm, and when we get out of rhythm, that's when we get into trouble." - Babatunde Olatunji, percussionist

Stress is also a big factor in dis-ease. Stress compromises the immune system as well as the nervous system. Common among many people who are stressed out are physical symptoms like skin disorders and rashes, chronic pain, digestive issues and headaches. If you look at the symptoms as an alarm system, you can diagnose your issues at their root cause instead of putting a bandaid on them.

The more you connect with the infinite power of the soul, the more healing energy you will generate. In the same way you can tap into the flow of creativity, you can tap into this flow of healing energy and share it with others. This is why visual art, music, dance and other disciplines are considered to be healing as both observable and occupational arts.

Healing happens when you face the "issues in your tissues" and start to make changes in your life that support a healthier and happier you. Making choices that bring you energy and vitality instead of

making choices that deplete or stress you, put you on the path to self-healing. Everything has to happen within you. When you have the experience of the flow of divine healing energy in YOU, then and only then can you can begin to share the healing energy with others.

I sometimes get a sensation in my hands; they start to vibrate and then get very hot. I can feel a flow of energy coming through the top of my head, down my arms and into my hands. I have come to learn that my hands do this when there is someone nearby or with me that is in need of healing. Now, if i am in public space, I can't really broadcast to a crowd that I have healing energy coming into my hands and it will go to waste if I don't put them on someone right away! But I can focus on the energy flow and discreetly share it with whoever needs it in the crowd. This happens a lot when I am teaching yoga and I do something similar to what I just explained. But if I am with a small group of people or with one person, I might ask if it would be okay if I put my hands on where healing is needed. I have found that the healing energy only gets activated when there is healing needed.

"When a person prays to the merciful Lord, he is extending himself outside, but the reaction is happening inside. Every action has a reaction, equal and opposite. You may pretend you are praying to the heavens, but actually you are changing yourself inside. It is you who are changing. When you are blessing the sick, you beg of the Almighty, but actually you are not begging for anything, because from inside your being, energy is pouring into the other person. It is from a state of compassion, of compassionate meditation, that the healing activity of God, within the being, flows."

The natural healing mechanism is very simple to use and you don't have to be a professional "healer" to use it. Both water and food have the capacity to be vessels and implements of healing. Just think… you can promote healing in yourself or in others by blessing a glass of water or eating high prana food as medicine instead of taking pharmaceuticals. Your health depends on the balance and rhythm of prana, your life force energy. When the rhythm of prana is out of order, then you are out of order. Your breath and the way in which you manage this vital force is crucial to health and the way you experience your life.

The amount of doubt you have regarding your own healing is in direct relation to the amount of suffering you have; to believe in the power of your own healing is a powerful tool for conquering the dis-eases of the body, mind and spirit. Healing is a form of creativity whose inflow is a personal and universal rhythmic order; the impact of which restores the human system to it's most pure and balanced form. According to Yogi Bhajan:

"Those who send good vibrations out will receive them ten times over from the universe. You gain when you give. There is no need to pray for yourself - pray for others and the Creator will pray for you."

HEALING OF ART

As discussed in the last chapter, we are vibrational beings vibrating all the time and if we are out of sync or not vibrating at the frequency of optimal health, we will experience pain, dis-ease, dis-comfort. The original state of the whole creation is vibration and we are susceptible to heard and unheard sound frequencies on a cellular level. All these vibrations form a rhythm which has a tremendous influence over how we function; sound and music, for example have a direct influence on our moods and energy levels. We don't hear just through our ears; we "hear" the vibrations through our skin and our bones.

Using mantras are a great way to uplift any situation and playing mantras at night while you sleep is one of the most effective (and easiest ways) to change thought patterns, negative thinking, and to realign one's frequency to the healing LOVE creative vibrational rhythm pattern. For example, you can eliminate negativity both inside of you and in your environment by playing a mantra, even at low volume all the time in a corner of a room. (The mantra *Chattr Chakkr Vartee* is a good one for that). If you play healing mantras for yourself and/or others, **they will heal.**

Once, a while back when I went in for a rather serious surgical procedure, I asked my doctor if, when under the knife, I could listen to "my" healing mantra. He gave me a plastic baggie with a red cross on it for my cd player, I plugged in my ear phones, and off I went. It helps to have a doctor that is open to this sort of thing. Recuperating in the hospital and at home, I played the Siri Gaitri healing mantra I'd been listening to - *Ra Ma Da Sa Sa Say So Hung* - continuously. My doctor had said that it would be at least two months before I could return to my "normal" life. When I went in for my post-op checkup about ten days later, he said that he had never seen anyone heal so fast from the operation I had.

Mantras work and sound healing really works, too … which is why sound baths using gongs and Tibetan singing bowls have become very popular as of late to aid in relaxation and meditation. Sound, music and rhythm have always been used to nourish and stimulate the theta brain frequencies that are commonly associated with deeper states of meditation; the heart rate slows down, the breath gets deeper and slower and it has a favorable overall healing effect on the entire body-mind-spirit. The gong, in particular is an extraordinarily powerful vehicle for transformation on any level, which is why we use it in Kundalini Yoga.

 "The gong is very simple. It is an inter-vibratory system. It is the sound of Creativity itself. The gong is nothing more, nothing less. Onewho plays the gong plays the universe. The gong is not an ordinary thing to play. Out of it came all music, all sounds, and all words. The sound of the gong is the nucleus of the Word."

The gong reorganizes the emotional energy in a person and can cause a a release of emotional blockages; so by releasing this tension some people may spontaneously cry, laugh, feel as if they are floating or leaving their body, or go into a deep sleep. The gong also impacts the physical body, the meridians and circulatory systems. It is completely possible that one strike of the gong can do the work of years and years of healing treatments or therapy.

Mandala is a Sanskrit word which means circle or completion. They are geometric representations of the universe, popular in all cultures, and considered to be traditional instruments of visual meditation. They are characterized by their geometric shape and symmetry; often representing layers of existence or awareness, and in the case of Tibetan Buddhist mandalas, a two-dimensional blueprint of a three-dimensional temple or palace (either real or imagined). Although the Tibetan Buddhist mandala is the one most people think of, there are mandalas in many different cultures and their purpose is to organize spiritual principles for use in meditation, ceremony, self-realization and spiritual healing.

The "sacred hoop", "medicine wheel", and "dream catcher" are just some of the mandala structures used by the Indigenous tribes of the Americas and to that you can add the Mayan Tzolk'in wheel and the Aztec sun stone! All of these mandala forms pre-date the Tibetan

Buddhist variety, but like all mandalas, are used for the same ceremonial, meditative and healing purposes.

Mandalas are works of art in any culture, but among the Tibetan Buddhists they are considered sacred works of art which represent the celestial residences of the Buddha or a meditational deity. The painting of mandalas in Tibet was a highly developed means of expression and important art form through which the entire Buddhist philosophy could be communicated. They were created to be used in temples and *monasteries and hung above altars to support Buddhist meditation and practice. Even today this highly treasured art form is taught in India at special schools for this type of meditative art practice.*

Some Buddhist monks are trained in the art of creating the ephemeral sand mandala. Through the three year-long artistic and philosophical training, a monk prepares themselves for the painstaking creative act (which can take up to several weeks) of making a *Dul-Tson-Kyll-Khor,* the "mandala of colored powders". The mandala is divided into four quadrants; each quadrant requiring the skills of one monk and their assistant. Starting in the middle and working outward, the group of four monks pour colored sand through special metal funnels or chak-pur, onto a table while they chant special mantras and prayers. It is said that this process produces powerful healing energies. After the sand mandala is completed, it is destroyed; an examples of the impermanence of all things - an important Buddhist teaching.

Celtic crosses, Labyrinth gardens, crop circles, and even Christian stained glass windows are all considered mandalas. Creating mandalas of your own, drawing or painting the symmetrical and concentric forms is said to be a very healing practice. Carl Jung discovered that the urge to make circular drawings often occurs at times of intense personal growth. He felt that it was evidence of the psyche's natural inclination to rebalance itself and the outcome being a better integrated personality.

Jung, who used circle drawings or mandalas, as he called them, in his work wrote:

"I sketched every morning in a notebook a small circular drawing, ... which seemed to correspond to my inner situation at the time. ... Only gradually did I discover what the mandala really is: ... the Self, the wholeness of the personality, which if all goes well is harmonious." - Carl Jung from Memories, Dreams and Reflections

The gong, when played correctly, creates a sonic rhythmic pattern which organizes your thoughts, your feelings, and your cellular structure so that illness or depression would find you a very uninhabitable environment. Mantras whether listened to or chanted, change your brain waves and blood chemistry when the pronunciation and rhythm is correct. If you don't know the mantra, just copying the sound current as you hear it creates the necessary rhythmic vibration for positive transformation and healing. A mandala used as a meditative focus can create a link to higher states of consciousness and self awareness. Creating your own mandalas can be used as a therapeutic tool to reduce stress and illness, depression, and to balance the hemispheres of the brain using it's symmetrical quartered structure as a template.

The successful healing outcome from using any and all art modalities in "art therapy" or "occupational therapy" is well documented. Giving yourself permission to make something just for the fun of it with no attachment to it's meaning or critical value, turning on some music and dancing to your heart's content, pure unedited automatic writing, storytelling and doodling are some things that even a professional artist, dancer, or writer or just about anyone can get tremendous healing benefit from.

One last bit of information on the power of self-imagined mandalas as a creative tool of self-discovery from the pen of Carl Jung:

"In 1938, I had the opportunity, in the monastery of Bhutia Busty, near Darjeeling, of talking with a Lamaic Rinpoche, Lingdam Gomchen by name, about the khilkor or mandala. He explained it as a dmigs-pa (pronounced ''migpa''), a mental image which can be built up only by a fully instructed lama through the power of imagination. He said that no mandala is like any other, they are all individually different. Also, he said, the mandalas to be found in monasteries and temples were of no particular significance because they were external representations only. The true mandala is always an inner image, which is gradually built up through (active) imagination, at such times when psychic equilibrium is disturbed or when a thought cannot be found and must be sought for, because it is not contained in holy doctrine." (Psychology and Alchemy, Princeton University Press)

YOU ARE WHAT YOU EAT - PINEAL REPAIR

A big part of The Yogic Art of Healing is having consciousness around what you put in your mouth. After all, as part of your creative inflow, you might consider what you eat to be a very important part of Creative Living.

Having sustainable energy, healthy elimination and a clear mind goes into being a productive and successful artist as well as a focused and disciplined spiritual practitioner. If you feel tired and unfocused, you can't get your work done. If you eat foods that are low in prana, like processed foods for example, you won't feel very sharp and your energy will wane quickly. If you eat foods that you don't eliminate within 24 hours, let's just say it..you shouldn't be eating it at all. If it hangs around in your stomach and intestines for more than 24 hours, it will create an unhealthy environment inside of you and believe me, you won't feel much like being creative or meditative.

I'm not going to dive deep into the yogic diet, but I will share some dietary tips, recipes and hacks that I have found to be fool-proof for general well-being, healing, quick energy, and system re-balancing. They mostly come directly from the Teachings of Yogi Bhajan and they will serve you well. But before I do that, let me tell you a little bit about the pineal gland.

The ancients have always been aware of this extraordinary and tiny sense organ located where the spinal cord and the brain meet. Believed to regulate sexual function, nerve and muscular strength, magnetic field frequency and extra-sensory perception, the yogis have always known of it as the location of the seventh chakra (a.k.a the crown chakra, thousand petalled lotus or tenth gate). In the 1940's, it was discovered that the pineal gland secreted a substance (seratonin) that regulated the intestinal wall muscles, controlled the clotting and flow of the blood and the action of the smooth muscle tissue, but most importantly (and especially for yogis and creatives) "opened the mind" and gave people something akin to religious experience.

The ancient yogis have always known that one must take good care of the pineal gland which is why they have been eating foods that are rich in serotonin like figs, bananas, banyan sap and the trinity roots: onion, garlic and ginger. One of the many healing benefits of yoga and meditation is the transformation of the spinal fluid into a more highly concentrated form of serum in the body. This is called "ojas" and it causes the pineal gland to secrete. Aside from aiding in the perception of higher states of consciousness, ojas are simply the best healing substance that we have.

The pineal gland can get calcified from chemicals in our modern world; for example from the fluoride in our water and in our toothpaste, as well as in food additives we blindly consume. A calcified pineal gland impairs sleep patterns, negatively affects cognitive abilities and reaction time, messes with our judgement and discernment, alters our perception and negatively affects performance.

We need the pineal gland to function well if we want to meditate deeply and be at our creative best. If the function of the pineal gland is limited, so are you. Just think how much more creative you could be if you improved your pineal gland function! Even though the pineal gland and other parts of the brain do become calcified with age, it can be reversed and it doesn't have to happen so early in life. Many ancient civilizations knew that the key to opening the doors of perception was the pineal gland, so if you believe in the "dumbing down" conspiracy theory, you could see why it would benefit the powers that be to have people functioning at only a portion of their potential.

Healing the pineal gland would involve eating foods and supplements that reverse pineal calcification such as avocados, almonds, beans, beets, chickpeas, hazelnuts and dates. Curcumin, the active ingredient in turmeric, can prevent and potentially reverse the damage from fluoride exposure. To minimize fluoride intake from public water, use fluoride filters. Of course, use fluoride-free toothpaste, and stay away from processed and pesticide-ridden foods (try to eat organic).

Here are some more consumables:

- Spirulina, chlorella and wheatgrass help to remove metal toxins, boost oxygen and immune function - which may decalcify the pineal.

- Raw cacao is high in antioxidants and helps to detoxify pineal gland.

- Iodine reduces the negative effects of fluoride.

- Apple cider vinegar and oregano oil both remove harmful organisms and metals; reducing the chances of pineal calcification.

- Tamarind paste eliminates fluoride through the urine.

YOU ARE WHAT YOU EAT - GOOD FOODS

The yogis divide foods into three groups: sun foods, earth foods, and ground foods. Sun foods, like fruits, nuts, avocados, dates, and coconuts, grow more than three feet off the ground. Because they absorb so much energy from the sun, they give you lots of quick, etheric energy and are perfect for when you feel the need to eat lightly and elevate your consciousness. They are also good for elders who tend to get bogged down with the heavier foods, and for heavy boned and slow moving people.

Earth foods grow in the earth; under the soil and have great energy from the earth and some energy from the sun, indirectly. Some of these are radishes, onions, garlic, ginger, beets, carrots, turnips, potatoes and other root foods, and peanuts. These foods are perfect for those who have nervous dispositions and need grounding. Earth foods are the most healing of the three food groups; they give you the kind of energy you need for physical work and worldly affairs. It's a good idea to eat more earth foods in the winter months or when it's cold outside because they fight infection.

Last are the vegetables and fruits that grow just above the surface; ground foods get most of their energy from the earth, a little less form the sun and are cleansing and very high in nutrients. Examples would be green vegetables, breads, beans and rice.

Yogi Bhajan said that food is the medicine which creates equilibrium. Eating balanced food that does not put a strain on the body creates a healing environment and if you eat sustaining foods, you'll have joy in your life. Food that stresses your body will destroy you.

Here are some healing foods that will never let you down:

TRINITY ROOTS

Onions, Garlic and Ginger are three roots that are essential for producing and sustaining energy in the body as well as for cleansing. If you want to have a potent, vital and creative life then you should include these roots in your diet.

- The onion was revered by the Egyptians and considered to be a symbol of the universe. For ages, onions and onion juice have been used to cure colds, fever, laryngitis, warts, earaches and cancer. Onions purify and stimulate the production of the blood, and is great for balancing blood sugar, and is a great anti-inflammatory food. Because it's so good at attacking bacteria, I eat raw onions as a precautionary measure before I travel and at the first sign of a sore throat or cold. It works! In cases of high fever that must be brought down quickly or in cases of extreme toxicity, massage the feet with half an onion. Yup…it really works!

- Garlic has always been considered a sacred and powerful healing herb. Great for gastrointestinal problems, typhus, cholera, bacterial infections, cancer and septic poisoning, garlic and its extract/oil is considered by Soviet doctors to be "Russian penicillin". Garlic increases and stimulates the production of semen which is why some religious sects (that require celibacy) forbid its consumption.

- Ginger was at one time recommended as a prevention against the plague! Ginger is considered to be medicine as well as a spice and is used as a digestive stimulant and to dispel nausea. A cup of ginger tea is so good after a meal. Ginger is the first thing recommended to pregnant women when they have morning sickness. When i was pregnant, I craved ginger ale but of course it has so much sugar in it; I put chunks of ginger in sparkling mineral water and let it sit for a while. Bingo.. worked like a charm!

Ginger is also good for menstrual cramps, nourishes the nervous system and allow the nerve channels to handle more energy, keeps the spine and cerebrospinal fluid healthy, promotes circulation and treats phlegm in the lungs accompanied with cough.

Do you ever get exhausted in the afternoon? Take three slices of raw ginger and chew them up for a few minutes; be sure to swallow the juice and discard the fibers. You'll get an instant nervous system pick-me-up. It works well when you are working on a project and need to push through or if you are getting tired from driving. If you are making fresh juice, be sure to add some fresh ginger juice to the mix. Great for overall energy and your immune system.

Trinity roots can be eaten separately, but when combined, have a synergistic effect. They are the basis of many an Indian curry and recipe, including kitcheree (mung beans and rice).

Jalapeno Milkshake

3-5 raw jalapeños, 8-10 oz milk, a little honey (cuts down the heat of the jalapeños * Put ingredients into a blender. Blend for 20-30 minutes. Pour into a glass and sip it. DO NOT drink it straight down. "The spirit will go through you." In fact, it's good to take it one spoon at a time. For a trouble-free life and it's delicious!

MUNG BEANS AND RICE WITH VEGETABLES

(KITCHEREE)

MAKES 8 SERVINGS

INGREDIENTS

- 1 cup mung beans
- 1 cup basmati rice
- 9 cups water
- 6-7 cups fresh vegetable
- ¼ Cup Ghee or olive oil
- 4-5 Cloves of fresh Garlic, crushed in a press
- 2 Onions, Chopped
- 1 finger fresh Ginger root, peeled and minced
- 1 1/2 Tsp Tumeric
- 1 1/2 Tsp Cumin powder
- 3/4 Tsp Ground Coriander seed
- Seeds of 5 Green Cardamon Pods (or 3/4 tsp powder)
- 1 Tsp Black Pepper
- ½ Tsp Crushed Red Chilies (more if you like spicy OR omit completely if you don't like it hot)
- 1 – 1 1/2 Tbsp Sea Salt

KITCHEREE COOKING INSTRUCTIONS

Rinse the mung beans and rice. Add the mung beans to boiling water and cook until they begin to split. Add the rice and cook another 15 minutes, stirring occasionally. Now add the vegetables.

Heat the ghee/oil in a sauté pan and add the onions, garlic, and ginger and sauté until clear. Add the spices and cook 5 more minutes, stirring constantly. This is the masala mixture. Add a little water if necessary. Add this to the cooked rice and beans. You can substitute vegetables as you like, as well as use Bragg Liquid Aminos, tamari, or soy sauce instead of salt. Tastes great with yogurt!

I like to cook the pot with a 1/2 lemon...shell included!

COMMENTS: A perfectly balanced dish, kitcheree is easy to digest and very satisfying. It is good any time of the year, but is perfect in the winter because it is so warming and filling. Because it is basically "pre-digested", it is excellent to use as a cleansing or healing mono diet. It is nourishing for the kidneys, aids in meditation, helps with constipation, and improves colon and digestive health. Mung beans, being so easy to digest, will give you your vegetarian protein without the digestive disturbance you might get from other beans. If you ever need to give your digestive system a reboot or heal an upset stomach, try eating kitcheree and Yogi Tea for a week or two.

Yogi tea is a delicious, healthful substitute for coffee or strong, black tea. It can give you a lot of energy from the synergy of ingredients (not from caffeine) and can make you feel alert and positive. When regularly included in the diet, it helps correct damage done to the nervous system by drugs and diseases of the nerves. It will improve your memory and balance you out when you're feeling out of balance. It can take away tiredness, discouragement, and depression. Yogi tea is both a remedy and a preventive measure for colds, flu, and diseases of the mucous membranes... PLUS it's delicious.

Make at least 4 cups at a time-one is never enough! For each cup use:

10 ounces water
3 cloves (for the nervous system)
seeds of 4 green cardamom pods (for the colon)
4 whole black peppers (a blood purifier) 1/2 stick cinnamon (for the bones)
1 slice ginger root (for the nervous system, colds, flu, and physical weakness)

1/4 teaspoon black tea (to catalyze the other ingredients)
1/2 cup milk (to prevent irritation to the colon and stomach) Boil the spices for 10-15 min. Add the black tea and steep for 2 min. Add milk, then reheat to the boiling point, remove immediately from the stove, and strain. Add honey to taste.

GREENDIET

A rebuilding diet that alkalinizes the body, is good for losing weight, it clears the skin, cleanses the liver, and relieves toxic mucus conditions. If you take this "diet" on, expect to feel vitalized and clear. 40 days of JUST green foods: salads, steamed greens, avocados, sprouts, mung beans, green fruit, etc. If it's green, it's okay (Yogi Tea throughout the day is recommended) To end the fast, add fruit, then grains, then dairy.

YOU ARE WHAT YOU EAT - HEALTHY TIPS

You can put foods into two categories: nutritious foods and sustaining foods. If you are looking for energy and strength, eat **nutritious foods.** These consist of easily assimilated whole, fresh and natural foods. You are going to want to eat **sustaining foods** if you are healing the body and want to maintain a state of health. What makes a food "sustaining" is the combination of nutritional content, it's preparation, the texture, taste, and smell, and the medicinal effect on the body. If you eat a combination of nutritious and sustaining foods, you will build a great foundation for Creative Living.

Eating a combination of raw and cooked foods is recommended; the roughage in raw vegetables will clean out and maintain health in your stomach and intestines and cooking foods will unlock the nutrients that are "trapped" in the molecules of the vegetables. If you are interested in digging deeper into the subject of eating for health, I highly recommend books on Ayurveda (the Indian science of healing). My favorite is Yogi Bhajan's *Foods for Health and Healing.*

And last but not least, most of these are Yogi Bhajan's rules for healthy eating and preparation of food:

1. Prepare and serve your food with love and care try to eat in a calm environment. Eating "on the run" or standing at the kitchen counter is not the most optimum way to eat.

2. Bless your food, be in gratitude, and eat consciously.

3. Eat to live, don't live to eat

4. Avoid snacking between meals and eat fewer meals. Eat only when you are hungry, not when the clock says its time to eat.

5. Chew your food well.

6. When you are three-fourths full, stop eating. You need to leave room for digestion.

7. Rest after every meal. You need to digest.

8. Don't eat after sunset if possible.

9. You should only be eating what you can eliminate in 18-24 hours.

10. You are what you eat.

STRESS

Stress is a huge problem in our society and living with high levels of anxiety is a lifestyle that many people have adjusted themselves to. Coping with the chaos of stress wears down our energy reserve and our immune system; stress being a root cause of heart failure, high blood pressure, and cancer. It impacts how we sleep or we don't sleep at night and as a result, how alert we are during the day. We make food choices based on our stress levels; for example under-eating or over-eating for emotional reasons or heading for comfort food when we feel uncomfortable. Stress also affects how we digest the food we eat; the more relaxed we are, the better our digestion will be.

Have you noticed that when you are stressed out, your relationships are affected, too? How can you be patient, compassionate and kind with others when you are nervous and edgy? Don't you find that stress puts you in a desperate state of mind? I am sure you have made some of your worst decisions when you were under stress or pressure. Being in that state of mind is also an invitation to resort to negative and self-destructive habits which isn't good for anyone.

If you can decrease or remove stressors from your life, then you are on the road to living a stress-free life. When I was younger I used to thrive on the adrenaline rush of doing things at the last minute, but I can no longer handle that kind of pressure. I've had to work on my time management skills and build up my energy reserves in order to handle and meet deadlines and project challenges. The adrenals, the kidneys, the immune and nervous systems are all directly impacted by stress so yogic-ly speaking, it would be beneficial to practice yoga sets and meditations that strengthen any or all of these…and believe me, there are plenty to chose from in the Teachings of Yogi Bhajan. The same can be said of the breath patterns that reduce stress; its good to have some stress-reducing pranayama on hand.

Let's face it, stress is a part of life, but HOW you react to the stress is going to determine your health, wellness, and your relationship to the creative flow. I don't know about you, but it's difficult to be creative when I am stressed out. Having awareness of what I like to call my "stress threshold" - in other words, knowing when stress becomes unhealthy for me is number one. Then I need to know how to turn the dial down on the inflow of stressors and which tools work for me; that's number two. And number three is that I need to know how I can fortify those depleted systems in my body so that they get stronger, give me an extra edge, and help with stress-resistance. And finally, number four, is that I actually have to do it. All of this is part of the self-analyzation process of being a creative and healthy human being I was talking about a few chapters back!

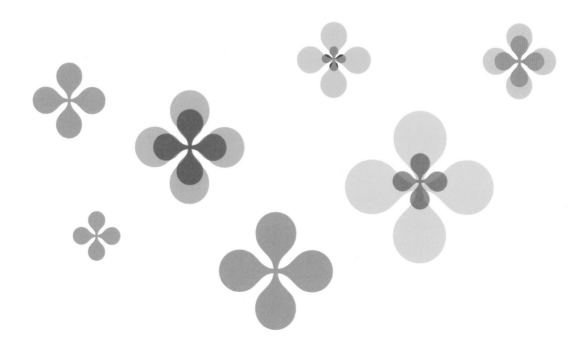

To review, there are three things that directly affect our stress level; diet, exercise, and the ability to maintain a meditative or neutral mind. If you can come up with the "right" combination of practices to support your equilibrium, you will not succumb to the negative effects of stress. But if you find that you are under stress, be sure to include vitamins C, A, D, E and the B complex, in your diet - all of which boost the system to handle stress. It is also recommended to take extra calcium, phosphorus, magnesium, copper and iron. Some of the best anti-stress foods include bananas, almonds, milk, honey, broccoli, spinach, wheat germ, sunflower seeds, and raisins. And of course, besides no white sugar, salt or nicotine… stay away from caffeine because it will just make it all worse.

HEALING, CREATIVITY AND SHUNIYA

Sat Nam Rasayan® is an ancient healing art practiced by many in the Kundalini Yoga community. Very much like tuning into the creative flow, once you learn how to access and surrender to healing energy, its flow will begin to serve you and others. With Sat Nam Rasayan®, as well as with Kundalini Yoga, pure consciousness and the healing process have neither boundary nor limitation. Therefore all aspects of the mind, body and spirit can be addressed.

Practitioners of Sat Nam Rasayan® (which means "healing in the true identity") believe that the meditative mind is our natural state of mind; we are all born with it, the cultural and familial conditioning starts right away, and soon enough, we "forget" who we really are. Discipline is the only way to undo the conditioning and to get back to our natural state of observing the world around us. You could say that through disciplined meditation, the healer opens up the neutral space so that healing energy can help the participant to open, stabilize and heal themselves. The *healer and participant are collaborators in this healing modality; sharing in the pure meditative absorption of shuniya or "zero".*

Shuniya is not particular to Sat Nam Rasayan®- all yogic practice (and art practice for that matter) aims to attain that most elevated state of pure consciousness, total awareness and nothingness through which all that is needed or desired flows. I'm talking about prosperity, creative "ideas", unconditional love, as well as healing energy. If you haven't figured out by now, anything you do or receive that is born from pure consciousness is pure healing energy. By the way, the ego has nothing to do with healing, shuniya, or the original you.

"So the first principle of a teacher is, 'I am not.' If you cannot practice shuniya, you cannot be a teacher of Kundalini Yoga. Shuniya means zero. The moment you become zero, then all powers will prevail through you. The power of a teacher of Kundalini Yoga is in his zero, in his shuniy. In shuniya you become zero, you reduce everything to nothing: 'I am nothing. Everything is nothing. There's nothing to be nothing.' The moment you become that, then everything radiates from you."

Shuniya is described as a calm state of awareness where the mind is brought to complete stillness and perfect harmony. It's a state of neutrality and non-reaction. There is no judgement, no good or bad, no wanting anything more or anything less; complete contentment with what is. From the state of shuniya, you don't have to try to do anything because everything will unfold naturally. You create the empty space and just allow. This quiet internal peaceful state allows for the original you "to be". It allows for self-healing, self-knowledge and self-realization and the flow of pure creativity.

Healing and creative energy are basically the same; they originate from the same place and you can use similar practices to access them. Even though it is a comprehensive system that many people swear by, Sat Nam Rasayan® is not the only practice that gives one access to healing energy. In fact, I have found that the more creativity I am generating, the more access I have to my healing ability. By talking to practitioners who are artists themselves, I have found that the discipline of Sat Nam Rasayan® is also a successful tool for opening up creative spaces.

If connecting to the Universal Mind is your game and the goal is attaining a state of shuniya through which your original self can shine, then I believe that the healing/creative flow will find you. Whether you act as an intermediary or a beneficiary of these flows, the result is the return to the original creative you.

Bring healing to all you do and all you know.

"PEOPLE ASK ME 'WHAT DO YOU THINK ABOUT WHEN YOU'RE IMPROVISING?' I'M TRYING TO GET MY MIND BLANK. I DON'T WANT TO THINK. THAT'S THE WHOLE POINT OF MUSIC. MUSIC HAS NOTHING TO DO WITH THINKING. IT'S SOMETHING WHICH YOU FEEL. YOU DON'T THINK, THERE'S NO TIME TO THINK   WHEN YOU'RE PLAYING. SO,
OUTSIDE OF SOME
SUPERFICIAL BEGINNINGS
WHEN I'M PLAYING, ONCE I GET PASSED THAT, YOU KNOW WHEN I'M REALLY PLAYING AT MY BEST, AS I'VE OFTEN SAID, WHICH IS NOT AS MUCH AS I'D LIKE IT TO BE, BUT I'M NOT THINKING ..THERE'S NOTHING TO THINK ABOUT. THEN YOU ARE TRYING TO GET INTO ANOTHER SPHERE. YOU KNOW, YOU DON'T WANT TO BE HERE THEN, YOU WANT TO GET SOMEPLACE ELSE SO MAYBE TAKE PEOPLE THERE. YOU DON'T WANT TO BE DOWN HERE THINKING ABOUT A EQUALS B AND B EQUALS C... THAT'S OVER NOW. SO NO, I DON'T THINK WHEN I'M PLAYING. IS MUSIC MEDITATION FOR ME? IT IS MEDITATION FOR ME DEFINITELY, YEAH, MUSIC IS MEDITATION FOR ME, YEAH. MUSIC IS MEDITATION." - SONNY ROLLINS

ART OF HEALING HIGHLIGHTS

1. Healing is the process of returning to balance. It is neither a cure nor an end result.

2. Healing is process-based continuous action.

3. Both creativity and healing are pure expressions of your soul; they need to cultivated to that they can shared or delivered.

4. Because the body and the mind are so deeply interconnected, the body will alert you to deeper emotional or psychic issues that need to be addressed. LISTEN.

5. Belief in your own healing ability is the most powerful tool for conquering the dis-eases of the body, mind and spirit. TRUST. Healing is a form of creativity whose inflow is a personal and universal rhythmic order; the impact of which restores the human system to it's most pure and balanced form.

6. Yogi Bhajan said that food is the medicine which creates equilibrium. Consciousness about the healing power of food is crucial.

7. Did you know a calcified pineal gland impairs sleep patterns, negatively affects cognitive abilities and reaction time, messes with our judgement and discernment, alters our perception and negatively affects performance? Did you know that flouride calcifies the pineal gland? And you still want to brush you teeth with fluoride toothpaste?

8. Let's face it, stress is a part of life, but how you react to the stress is going to determine your health, wellness, and your relationship to the creative flow.

9. Having awareness of your "stress threshold" - when stress becomes unhealthy for you- is important. How do you turn the stress dial down? Which tools work for you?

10. What can you do to fortify those depleted systems in your body so that you get stronger, have an extra edge, and have more stress-resistance?

11. If connecting to the Universal Mind is your game, then I believe that the healing/creative flow will find you.

12. Mantras, mandalas, the gong, automatic writing, and doodling- yes doodling - can all be used as healing modalities.

13. "Whether you are healthy or sick, there is no separation between you and God. When you are healthy, you are the health. When you are sick, you are the disease. There is nothing beyond you; there was never anything beyond you, and there shall be nothing beyond you; provided you believe in yourself. If you have rhythm within, then you have found reality. When there is no rhythm within, when you don't listen to your own heart beat, how can you listen to the heart beat of others? All charity begins at home. If you have not loved your Self, how can you love somebody else? If you don't keep yourself clean, how can you appreciate anyone else's cleanliness? This is the secret of ease and disease."

BREATH of TEN MEDITATION TO BECOME DIS-EASE FREE

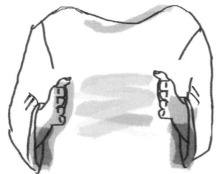

THIS PRANAYAM IS A MAGNETIC ENERGY THERAPY. THE ENERGY CONNECTION BETWEEN THE HANDS MUST NOT BE BROKEN.

IT CAN GIVE YOU A DISEASE-FREE BODY and a CLEAR MEDITATIVE MIND and Develop your INTUITION BUT it Requires practice!

POSTURE: EASY POSE WITH A STRAIGHT SPINE

FOCUS: Concentrate on the energy you feel between the palms of your hands.

TIME: To put all the Chakras in rhythm, do this meditation every day for 11 minutes. You can gradually increase the time to 16½ minutes

MUDRA: Your eLBOWS are bent and your forearms and hands are relaxed in a clapping position at the level of the SOLAR PLEXUS. Your hands move IN and out as if you are clapping BUT THEY DO NOT TOUCH. Stop the inward motion when hands are about 6-8 inches apart. MOVE SLOWLY and Rhythmically.

BREATH:

The breath is timed with the movement of the hands. Each stroke of the breath is one complete clapping motion. (hands move IN, hands move out) INHALE 5 STROKES through the NOSE WITH 5 complete CLAPPING MOTIONS. THEN EXHALE IN 5 STROKES through the mouth as you Do the NExt 5 clapping motions. CONTINUE... DO NOT BREAK the RHYTHM oF Breath + movement.

TO END: INHALE HOLD BReath foR 20 SECONDS as you press your hands against your face as hard as you can. EXHALE. INHALE AGAIN HOLD FOR 20 Seconds as you press your hands strongly against your HEART center. EXHALE. INHALE ONE LAST TIME and HOLD FOR 20 SECONDS as you press your hand against your NAVEL Point. EXHALE & RELAX.

ART OF SELF-CARE

A DIVINE RESPONSIBILITY

"When you know who are you, what are you, how you are, how you are. What is your frequency is, what your potential frequency is, what your sensitive frequency is, what your projection of infinity of psyche is, what rate of psyche is, at what frequency your psyche is doing, how much you are, how much you are not. I mean to say, do you have any measurement of yourself? You know, it's a beautiful wonderful body, it's not something of a joke."

Creative Living thrives on self-care.

We are all by nature loving, prosperous, and creative beings and to that end, we must acknowledge this truth from the inside out. In our lives, many of us are taught that we are broken and must be fixed or that what we need to make us whole can be obtained from the outside. While the Universal Mind is an energy field that we uplink to and download from, we are self-generating, self-healing, and self-renewing beings in a direct and constant relationship with the infinite flow. If healing is a form of creativity whose inflow is a personal and universal rhythmic order, the impact of which restores the human system to it's most pure and balanced form, then the art of self-care nourishes that personal rhythmic order so that love, prosperity and creativity can flood our lives.

Self-care returns you to that perfect ecstatic state, but it also involves figuring out who you are.

Self care can mean taking time out for yourself or adjusting your life to minimize stress and maximize joy; it could take the form of "filling the well" (think Julia Cameron in *The Artist's Way*) and/or putting aside the time to play and have fun. In terms of creativity, I would like to suggest that self-care means familiarizing yourself with the body-mind-spirit operational system and figuring out how to integrate it into your particular physical and auric configuration so that you can experience the most joyous and natural creativity possible.

"If you have the strength, you have the wisdom, you have the knowledge, you have the character, you have the power to deliver, you have your honesty for yourself, you have your truth for yourself, you have love and respect and self-esteem for your self, you are okay. These are the real things"

SELF-CARE BASICS

Prana, Apana, and Udayana. Yogi Bhajan said that our life was governed by these energies that make the physical body act and react; all faculties being based on the balance or imbalance of these powers. Prana give you energy and asana takes away what is not needed by you. Udayana maintains you. The ancients call these energies "vayus" or air currents: prana, asana and udayana being just three of the five major vayus in the human body.

Prana resides in the chest region and is linked to the taking in of life force energy through the breath and asana is located in the area below the navel and governs all processes of elimination. Udayana operates from the throat upward into the head region and controls speech, projection, and all things mental…including your memory.

The Kundalini energy rises when the pranic and apanic forces mix at the navel (as the result of specific breath or physical exercises) and through the assistance of the third vayu, udayana, is brought up from the bottom of the spinal column to the top into the tenth gate. Yogi Bhajan said that keeping these three major vayus balanced and flowing is crucial to our physical and mental health.

One of the most essential tasks in self-care is learning about how this energy works and keeping it in balance. If you don't have enough energy, you need to work with the pranic force. If you are holding on to things and can't let go, you need to work with the apanic force. If you are disorganized, overwhelmed and scattered, you need to work with the *udayanic* force.

"If you can control these three vayus, the rest of the vayus will automatically come into alignment. According to the ancient scientific facts, the entire functioning of the body is not muscular and is not nervous, either. It is by those airs."

We do all sorts of things to make ourselves feel pampered yet we seldom concentrate on the basics when thinking about how to administer self-care. Being creative is not unlike driving a fine car, yet many of us go as far as we can without re-fueling or changing the oil. Have you ever looked under the hood to see how the machinery works? We just put our foot on the accelerator and go …and go… and go until we run out of gas or something is out of rhythm.

There are, of course, different kinds of self-care; physical, emotional, spiritual, creative, intellectual, social, and sensory. And depending on your particular needs, there will always be something you can do (or not do) that will make you feel like you are taking care of yourself. While getting a massage or a spa treatment is a great way to administer self-care, there are so many other ways to nurture your soul.

For example, physical self-care might include some form of daily exercise or yogic practice; definitely something that you enjoy doing. It would include eating delicious nutritious, sustaining foods and maybe drinking freshly juiced fruits and vegetables. It could include getting the sleep you need, resting when you feel tired, and treating yourself to a massage. It might also include not eating, drinking or doing things that you know your body doesn't do well on…and we all know how challenging that can be sometimes.

Self-reflection is a big part of emotional self-care which might include checking in with your feelings and processing them. You can do that through journaling, meditation, dancing, taking walks, being creative, volunteering or just doing something nice for someone else. NOT burying emotional triggers and issues, but instead dealing with them, is a humongous component of emotional self-care.

Intellectual self-care might involve reading, researching or satisfying your curiosity about a subject that interests you; you might consider learning a new skill or language, pursuing something that challenges your mind, engaging in stimulating conversations, watching documentaries or panel discussions, and even taking a course or going back to school. The idea is to nourish the mind and feed your interests.

Social self-care would involve spending time with people you love, connecting with old friends, or indulging in the art of conversation with someone you don't know. Collaboration, working in community and other social engagements taps into the soul's desire to merge with others. If you are involved in a spiritual practice, you could spend time or be of service in your spiritual community, congregation or sangat. If you are an artist, going to gallery openings, museums and making/having studio visits are great ways to nourish social connections with like-minded people.

"It's a natural process to grow. It's a natural process to die every day. It's a natural process to age...but it's a personal matter to become a sage. It's a personal... it's not a natural process. Because your all knowledge and all wisdom is when you are born. As a child, you have a perfect psyche, you have a perfect innocence and you are in ecstasy; that you will never get. That's gone. That's gone! To regain that, you need a very intensive self-care. To regain that you need very self and very self inner core. To regain that you need that joy inside YOU."

SELF-CARE AND SELF-DISCIPLINE

How do you get that joy back inside of YOU? You can develop the physical body so that you have the strength to go and do and get the things you want. You can also develop the radiant body so that you are electrically charged and magnetic and everything will come to you. The ideal method is to develop both of these strengths so that you can change gears as you see fit. Your mind will be under your control and you will be able to manage and direct your energy. You won't be a slave to your emotions or to the exterior conditions of your environment. You'll be a genuinely joyous self-sustaining you.

"Most people do not understand the value of self-discipline. It is like having a car with no brakes and no steering wheel and believing you are driving! Life does not mean anything if you have not enjoyed it. Many people have the capacity, intelligence, privilege, environments and stature in life, but they do not enjoy self-discipline. They are wandering within themselves."

No matter what you are or what you do- an artist, a healer, a lawyer, a concert pianist - you need to practice self-nourishing rituals on a regular basis. Through self-discipline and consistency, you can take yourself from average to sensational in a relatively short amount of time.

Since I am a yogi and an artist, I have experienced the effects of self-discipline on my own well-being and professional advancement. I know that self-discipline can give you strength, power, self-confidence and projection. Meditation and a regular spiritual practice will give you the grace and altitude you need to navigate life's challenges. And it connects you to your higher self/soul so that everything you do is infused with the creative flow that is the Kundalini energy itself.

Doesn't matter if you are uplinking to the Universal Mind or preparing to deliver a project, your success in life depends on your self-discipline. Self-care is all about personal sustainability and this is only possible by increasing promoting habits and decreasing demoting ones. It is also important to set reasonable goals and outcomes so that the stress of not reaching them doesn't hijack your creativity.

Maintaining a level of consistency is the key to successful self-care. A daily yogic practice or sadhana is the highest form of self-care. Here are four yogic practices you can do daily. This teaching will take you far.

1. Breathing consciously (pranayam) nurtures a relationship with Divine Consciousness.

2. Chanting mantra is, according to Yogi Bhajan, "the mental vibratory projected thunderbolt of the human" and has the supreme power of making the mind and the neutral self one and the same.

3. Meditation will clear your subconscious mind so you can think straight.

4. Yogic exercise changes the blood chemistry and opens up the channels to receive and direct the creative flow. *"Some people misunderstand about yogic exercises. Yogic exercises are not physical exercises at all, they do not mean anything physical, except they are tune-ups. Yoga exercises are meant for glandular system because glands are the guardians of the health."* - Yogi Bhajan

Self-care is living in a conscious and responsible way so that you can flourish; making sure you get what you need to grow and function at your best all of the time. I am not talking about a "one-off" creative spiritual experience; I am talking about aligning yourself with Conscious Creativity for the long term.

Your self-care regimen might start with asking yourself some crucial questions…Do you take responsibility for your inflow and outflow, in other words, your prana and apana? What are you listening to? What are you saying? What do you eat and how do you eat it? When and how do you eliminate it? Do you have a yoga and meditation practice? If not, what are you doing to move the body and settle the mind? Are you getting enough sleep? Do you spend time with people who nourish you or deplete you? What do you do for work and is it fulfilling? What do you do for leisure? Do you even have time for leisure? Are you mitigating your stress levels? Does your lifestyle support your cycle of life? Are you paying attention to the changes that your body goes through as you get older? Are you processing your emotions in a healthy way?

Another way to administer self-care is to de-toxify. I'm not just talking about going on a juice fast or throwing out your microwave, I'm talking about eliminating toxic and negative thinking, leaving or removing toxic relationships, and finding healthier work situations to be in. Stress is toxic so aiming for less stress in your life is a form of detoxification, too.

In a nutshell, the choices you make can and will serve your health, vitality, prosperity and creativity. Yogi Bhajan taught exactly how to achieve this by advocating daily activities like getting up early in the morning before the sun rises to exercise and meditate (when pranic energy is at its maximum), taking cold showers to unclog the capillaries and organs, consciously breathing to prolong your life and neutralize your mind, chewing your food well to activate the youth-enhancing saliva, and many other actions that fit into the category of self-care.

"Creativity, when combined with physical and psychological concentration and meditation is very helpful. It balances the human energy and gives strength to the radiant body. This way prosperity and success come to people who, against all odds can smile; against all provocation can peacefully talk; and against all obnoxiousness can beautifully behave. They are bound to be very successful. There is no such thing as defeat for them."

SELF-CARE FOR CREATIVES

Artists have a tendency to work beyond their comfort zones; to ignore some of the most basic self-care essentials like getting enough sleep or eating for sustainability. Many artists and creatives, although there are exceptions, forgo their well-being to complete a project on time or they get lost in the timeless and spaceless labyrinth of creativity. Although these are relevant points for all, creatives should take heed.

1. Mind the body - artists tend to assume weird positions; reaching, bending or hunching over, over-using parts of the body and performing repetitive movements for extended periods of time. Tendonitis, carpal tunnel, back and neck pain are common chronic ailments for visual artists. Each artistic discipline has its own bevy of chronic ailments. Suggestions: take breaks throughout the day to stretch, move, change position. Set working limits. Drink water. Figure out a way to include exercise (or yoga) into your life. I know from experience that being in the intense focus of creativity overrides any pain or discomfort, so you must pay attention to what hurts, stretch, change position, and in other words, take a break.

2. Mind the mind - meditation or relaxing to quiet the mind is essential to keep everything in balance. A creative person's mind is always in motion and this can get mentally exhausting or confusing. If you don't clear the subconscious mind with meditation, there is just too much mental intrigue to deal with and if you are a creative person, you know what I'm talking about; let's just say that your attention is better spent on your creative process than on your creative drama. Many artists create in the privacy of their own work space and unless involved in collaborative projects, spend most of their time alone. That, in combination with an overactive and overcrowded

subconscious mind, is like an invitation to depression, anxiety and fear.

3. Mind the gut - It always comes back to what you eat. If you are not eating for energy, stamina and focus, you are just wasting the opportunity to fuel your creativity. So many artists get "sloppy" about what and when they eat, drink tons of coffee, and so on. You know the stories of dancers that starve themselves and smoke cigarettes to fit a physical ideal, or musicians that abuse alcohol and drugs because they think self-destructive habits are part of the package. There's no law that says an artist must abuse themselves! Nourish your body and mind the best way you know how; with healthy sustaining food in a relaxed atmosphere with the proper time to digest whatever you take in.

4. Mind the medium - Chemicals, toxic substances like paint mediums and thinners, paint made with cancer-causing pigments, and other deadly art supplies like resins, epoxies, sealers, lacquers should be avoided or special care taken to protect yourself (and others) from touching or inhaling them. Even though some dangerous art supplies have been discontinued, banned, or adjusted there are still plenty of them left that can do serious harm. Check labels and make sure, even if the materials are non-toxic, that there is adequate ventilation or wear a proper mask. Many artists who use dangerous materials feel that it is just the price they have to pay to be an artist…but that's a misguided myth …and also avoidable. Remember, art making does not have to be deadly to be good.

5. Mind the goals - What do you want in life and what are you willing to do to get there? There are so many levels to being a creative person: there's the work itself, the promotion of the work, the

financing of the work, the impact of the work and so on. In addition to figuring out your own artistic goals, most creative people have personal goals, too. And sometimes, but not always, artistic goals can be in conflict with personal goals. I guess what I am trying to say here is that you need to figure out who you are and that can only be done with introspection. Once you figure out what you want and what you are willing to do to get there, you have to determine and prioritize your goals; which ones are short-term and which ones are long-term? You'll have to set boundaries, which is crucial in all areas of self-care; you might have to decline invitations and opportunities and say "no" when you want to say "yes". This is just exercising compassion for YOU. Self-discipline comes in very handy here. *"If you don't know where you are going, you'll end up someplace else." - Yogi Berra*

6. Mind the resources - An artist has to analyze their resources before they embark on a project. Some of the resources I am referring to are energy, ability/talent, collaboration/assistance, time, and money. Anyone on this planet who wants to be successful in ANY field, must pretty much do the same. Do you have the energy to bring the project to completion? Do you have the ability or talent to do the project? Do you have the collaboration or assistance needed to deliver the project? Do you REALISTICALLY have enough time to do the project? And what will the project cost? Can you afford to it? Can you get funding? How much and from where? This self-examination is a big part of an artist's self-care. Even if the project is small, you still need to mind the time, the cost, and the energy expended.

7. Mind the fun - Yes, even artists and creatives need to have fun. Take time off to play. Intersperse your schedule with some down time.

You know how people always pad their estimates to cover unexpected expenses? Well, make sure that when you are creating your timetables and schedules that you figure in some time for you.

8. Mind the boundaries - the best word an artist, or anybody else for that matter, can learn to use is the word "no". We sometimes think we are doing something good for others when in fact, we are doing them and ourselves harm. In modern parlance it is called enabling. When you give a person what they need, in some cases, it is not to relieve their suffering but instead to relieve your own. We want to avoid feeling our own pain of experiencing someone else's discomfort …so in actuality, we are just doing it for ourselves. In our need to be liked, to avoid conflict and to appear compassionate, we end up doing this act of self-harm which Chögyam Trungpa called "idiot compassion".

"Idiot compassion is the highly conceptualized idea that you want to do good to somebody. At this point, good is purely related with pleasure. Idiot compassion also stems from not have enough courage to say no."

Creative and spiritual people are often seen as "sensitive and compassionate types" and so are often taken advantage of. That's why its so important to set boundaries with regard to due dates, time schedules, physical and mental exertion and getting paid. I can't tell you how many people I know who would rather cut into their own profit, their energy and their time than to inconvenience or upset a client or customer.

Saying "no" is a conscious act of self-care.

SUGGESTED PRACTICES

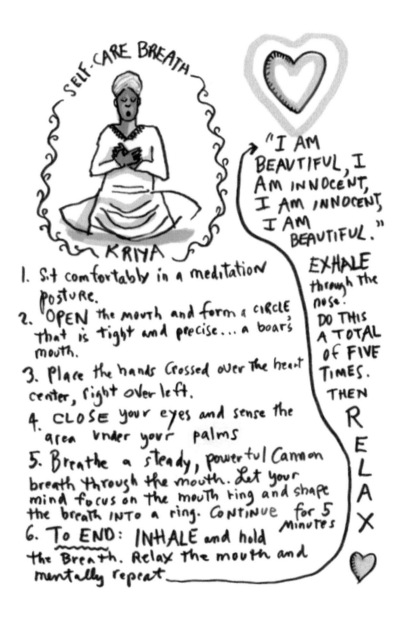

SELF-CARE BREATH

KRIYA

"I AM BEAUTIFUL, I AM INNOCENT, I AM INNOCENT, I AM BEAUTIFUL."

1. Sit comfortably in a meditation posture.
2. OPEN the mouth and form a CIRCLE that is tight and precise... a boar's mouth.
3. Place the hands crossed over the heart center, right over left.
4. CLOSE your eyes and sense the area under your palms
5. Breathe a steady, powerful cannon breath through the mouth. Let your mind focus on the mouth ring and shape the breath INTO a ring. CONTINUE for 5 minutes
6. TO END: INHALE and hold the Breath. Relax the mouth and mentally repeat_____

EXHALE through the nose. DO THIS A TOTAL OF FIVE TIMES. THEN RELAX

Self-care breath increases inner energy and strength, boosts the immune system and cleanses the body.

REJUVENATION MEDITATION
(11-31 minutes)

① SIT IN EASY POSE WITH STRAIGHT SPINE.

② ELBOWS RELAXED Bring HANDS PALMS UP to HEART LEVEL The little fingers of the 2 hands Touching along their length.

③ Other fingers + thumbs are spread apart.

④ LOOK AT THE TIP OF YOUR NOSE AND Beyond that into the earth.

⑤ Deeply inhale through semi-puckered mouth & hold the breath for 4-5 seconds. THEN completely exhale ALL the air from the lungs IN 4 EQUAL breaths through the NOSE.... mentally saying SA TA NA MA on the 4 strokes. Hold the breath OUT for 2-3 seconds, then continue the cycle.

✳ Begin with 11 minutes.... very slowly build your practice to 31 minutes; UNDER NO CIRCUMstances should the meditation be practiced for more than 31 minutes.

✳ This is a very powerful meditation. IT WORKS MAINLY ON GLANDULAR SYSTEM AND WILL give you strong health & excellent regenerative capabilities. BEST DONE BEFORE BED... CAN SPACE you out ✳ IF DONE IN THE DAY, give yourself plenty of time to "RECOVER".

"Caring for myself is not self-indulgence, it is self-preservation, and that is an act of political warfare."

~ Audre Lorde, warrior poet

The great enemy of creativity is fear. When we're fearful, we freeze up - like a nine-year-old who won't draw pictures, for fear everybody will laugh. Creativity has a lot to do with a willingness to take risks. Think about how children play. They run around the playground, they trip, they fall, they get up and run some more. They believe everything will be all right. They feel capable; they let go. Good businesspeople behave in a similar way: they lose $15 million, gain $20 million, lose $30 million and earn it back. If that isn't playing, I don't know what is!

- Faith Ringgold, artist and writer

ART OF PROSPERITY

WHAT CAN YOU SHARE?

WHAT ARE YOU GRATEFUL FOR?

Prosperity. Everybody wants it. And why not? It's a flourishing and thriving situation. Everybody loves to talk about how to get it but what does that word bring up for you? Money? An attitude of gratitude? Giving to receive? Your cup runneth over? If you hold a yoga class or a lecture on prosperity, you can bet your bottom dollar, people will come. Who doesn't want to know how to become prosperous, how to make more money, and how to be in the flow of abundance? Yogi Bhajan described prosperity as the *"transformation of the gross Earth onto the beautiful ether of the psyche of the Infinite."*

PROSPERITY BASICS

First and foremost, Prosperity is much more than just the acquisition of riches and second of all, it's not a state of affairs, it's a state of mind. The third truth is that prosperity, like creativity, is an energy flow. It's easy to access but it takes effort to maintain.

In fact, we all have a very weird relationship to prosperity. We want it, we are willing to work for it, we pray, we talk to spirit all the time when the circumstances are less than ideal but the minute we are prosperous, forget about it! We'll find a million other things to do than call on our soul.

"When you are in a pain and in a coercion and in a bad situation, you are very healthy because there is a challenge to meet, there is a sympathy in yourself, there is a time to excel, there is a time to achieve, there is time to do that. Moment your circumstances become into the just-border-case-of-prosperity, you fall apart. It is most difficult to handle prosperity. It is easy to handle adversity because when the circumstances are adverse, you call upon your soul, your spirit, your intelligence, you keep going. When things are prosperous, at that time you go nuts, because you think you made it. Actually, handling prosperity is more difficult than becoming prosperous. Living is more difficult than death, is that true or not?"

Think about it. When things are not going your way, you do your sadhana, you go to yoga class more often, you eat better foods, you meditate more, you clean up your act; in other words, you treat your yoga practice like medicine or a magic spell. Your challenges and obstacles lead you to your soul's journey which is a good thing… but when the problems disappear and things are good, you ease off on your practice because your think you don't "need" it as much. Why do we go deep in our practice when we are in a desperate situation? Why don't we go deep in our practice ALL the time so we can keep the prosperity flowing? It's because maintaining it is always much harder than achieving it.

That's why Yogi Bhajan said *"keep up and you'll be kept up"*. When people go on a weight loss regimen, part of their plan is actually called "maintenance". Why? Because it's basically easier to drop the weight than it is to keep the weight off after goal weight is achieved. Same with the state of prosperity; you can increase your radiance and energy field to attract it, hold it, and support the flow of it. But most important is to keep *it in gear and moving. Prana, Apana and Udayana - inflow, outflow and maintenance.*

"...when you look in adversity you will find out what adversity is. When you will find what adversity is, you solve it. Moment you solve adversity, there will be a prosperity."

A big part of prosperity is opportunity and when it comes, it often doesn't appear in the way you had imagined that it would. That's why you have to keep your heart open, your mind clear and your intuition on point. That way, you won't be tempted by false opportunity. That way, you won't miss a real opportunity when it comes. *Which brings us again to **maya**...*

Maya is the illusion of separateness. Because G.o.d. is our own inner consciousness and guidance system, when you feel separate, you feel lost. God and me, me and God are one is a good mantra to use when you feel this way. Maya is the thing that tests you by splitting your personality. You might feel worried because there are lots of things that come to harass or test you. You might feel at wit's end because you are faced with innumerable challenges. You might have set a standard of commitment for yourself and then a distraction comes to break your reserve.

Yogi Bhajan explained that maya comes to tell you how refined you are. *"Maya is a faculty to test your steel."* You'll find out soon enough that you can either cut through time and space or your can't. If you recognize maya for what it is... and can cut through, dissolve, overcome, and/or ignore it...then prosperity is on the other side. You could think of maya as a helpful tool for self-realization.

```
"Prosperity is a state of mind and it is extremely
bewitching. It puts spells on us. It is hypnotic. It's
our inner urge. Prosperity, prosperity, prosperity, we
dream, we think, we live to, we share, we compare, we
work. At what cost? We never understand. Prosperity
is for this Planet Earth and its maya --and mostly or
many times and all the time, all prosperity - it
takes away from reality, equal and opposite . Because
prosperity means, where we put our whole being to
make that prosperity our goal - whenever there is
anything in maya our goal - we neglect our soul. That
is how it is, it can never be wrong."
```

And number four is that prosperity involves the act of creative transformation. What do I mean by that? Just like taking dis-ease to healing, thought waves to ideas, and ideas to creativity, in order to take adversity to prosperity, it requires a bit of "alchemy".

As Above, So Below.

The common definition of alchemy is that it's a secretive ancient practice that seeks to turn lead into gold, although the transmutation of common metal into a precious substance was not the only goal of the practice. Alchemy was based in a spiritual system in which all things contain a universal spirit that is alive and well and growing in the earth. Since lead, a base or common metal was considered to be physically and spiritually immature, alchemists believed you could take lower vibrational substances and transform and refine them to spiritual perfection.

Even though alchemy was "born" in the year 100, it reached its popularity in medieval times. It was considered an art form that was both experimental and magical. The mythical substance called "the philosophers' stone" was reputed to be a substance that could heal, prolong life, and change ordinary substances into magical mystical gold.

Metaphorically speaking, your philosopher's stone is your radiance.

It gives you the power to transform lower frequencies into higher frequencies. You have the potential to become a radiant being so that you can connect with the universal radiance, thereby filling your life with creativity, awareness and opportunity. When adversity hits, think creatively. Ask your own inner consciousness and guidance system how to proceed when you feel separate and lost. Chances are, it will lead you to your radiant body...and your radiant body will take you to prosperity.

All of this takes us right back to radiance because prosperity will both come to you in radiance and it will be maintained by your radiance. In addition to prosperity and creativity, your radiance will give you protection, royalty and grace and will cut through karmic blocks and adversity.

"What is the secret of prosperity? Secret of prosperity is how you handle a trauma, a drama crisis, that is, that is the secret. Your intelligence, your degree, your well read personality, your well established personality, your obnoxious surroundings, your challenges, your, your pain and your gain and whatever you want to call it, is based on one thing only - how you handle a situation and each situation is a challenge in itself... so we walk and we grow everyday... we have grown today... we will grow tomorrow."

The most important thing about prosperity that I forgot to mention ...is that it wants to be shared. That's the nature of prosperity itself; to be overflowing with creativity, skills, talent, money, insight, love, or whatever gifts you have and to share them with others.

What do YOU have to share? Even if you don't think you have prosperity, i am sure that you have something going for you, or something you have plenty of that you could share with others. Do you have a skill or ability you can teach? Have you considered mentoring? If you have some extra time, perhaps you can do some volunteer work. Serving and helping others is the match that ignites community. Get a bunch of people together and have a prosperity circle in which each person has to bring a skill, a teaching, a talent to share with the group. Potlucks are the perfect way to share recipes and of course, meals and great conversation and why not create a community cookbook with anecdotes and personal histories? We can never build community if we are frantically holding on for dear life to what we have. We all do that to a certain degree as if our resources (whatever they might be) will never be replenished.

To be truly prosperous, you must open your heart and wish the best for others. To wish prosperity for just yourself and not to think about others is not prosperous thinking at all. Not creative thinking, either.

The more YOU give, the more you get. It's the same with praying… when you pray for others, you get the kickback.

RADIANCE - CREATIVE PROSPERITY'S BEST FRIEND

All the qualities that make you creatively prosperous are because of your radiance.

"When you understand who and what you are, your radiance projects into the universal radiance and everything around you becomes creative and full of opportunity."

Radiance comes up a lot in this book because it's so important in Creative Living. In earlier chapters, I wrote about the radiant body's relationship to inspiration, prana and the art of deliverance, and I described it as the "philospher's stone" - the mythical substance of healing and transmutation.

The radiant body is what Yogi Bhajan referred to as the "keep up spirit"…it is what you need to "deliver"; to take whatever you are doing to completion so you can share it, perform it, hang it, sing it, serve it, or whatever. When you feel like throwing in the towel, you need to call on your radiance to keep going…and radiance will improve your clarity and awareness when working on projects. Your radiance makes you stand out in a crowd; you may have heard it sometimes referred to as your charisma. It makes you limitless and fearless and as far as creative living goes, there is nothing that will transform the mundane into fabulous like a strong radiant body.

And now, I'd like to tell you about Guru Gobind Singh and his trusty falcon. The tenth Sikh Guru, who lived in 17th century India, was a great spiritual master, a courageous and undefeated warrior, a well respected poet and philosopher. With all these amazing gifts, he was the embodiment of true radiance. If you look at historical and lyrical paintings and drawings of Guru Gobind Singh, he was seldom depicted without his falcon or baaj. I wanted to know more about the relationship between the Guru and his falcon, so I started digging around in books and on the internet in hopes of finding some connection or metaphor to further advance my case about the influence of radiance on creativity.

It is said that Guru Gobind Singh's Baaj was not an ordinary falcon and many of the qualities and traits that Sikh parents wanted their children to embody were taught to them by teaching them stories about the falcon. These are traits that strengthening the radiant body will give you, and maybe not so coincidentally, the qualities and traits one must possess as a creative person. These values are:

1. Self-Reliance and Independence - the falcon hunts for what it needs to survive therefore we need to find a way to take care of own needs; in other words, no matter what we do as artists, we need to make a living . If there is something that an artist has plenty of it is faith. And so that one-pointed determination sometimes makes us forget that we have to make sure we've got our life covered...that we always remain "realistic". Yogi Bhajan said that Faith means one-pointedness of mind toward Infinity. It's important to cultivate a strong radiant body because it will help you to succeed in any thing you choose to do maintaining higher consciousness and connection with earthly matters.

2. Freedom- a falcon cannot be caged otherwise it will die- therefore we must not be enslaved by our circumstances or the limits we place on

ourselves. We must try to break through all obstacles in order to thrive as creatives. A strong radiant body give us the ingenuity and drive to figure out how to overcome challenges that come up. It's impossible to feel entrapped with a strong radiant body!

3. Humility - just like the falcon soars the skies and yet can see a tiny mouse on the earth, we must always keep our focus on earthly realities no matter how successful we may become. Our egos get us into trouble. The radiant body will keep us "real", will give us the self-containment and grace to be naturally humble.

4. Detachment - falcons never keep a permanent home and are always ready to fly away and explore; Inside of the creative mind, one must be ready to try new things, to experiment, and not be attached to what is "safe". The radiant body gives us that self-confidence not to be needy or worried when the unexpected happens or we are called upon to change direction in a creative project. Creativity does not "belong" to us but is a cosmic flow that everyone has access to.

5. Resilience- All birds fly in the direction of the wind, except for the falcon. As an artist you must be ready to fly against "the norm" or popular opinion. Life as an artist or creative is often a challenging one and you must learn how to take criticism and rejection. You MUST be resilient to be a creative person....Radiance will give you that. It gives you the ability to "roll with the punches"

6. Courage - Falcons are not afraid to go after something bigger than themselves... and neither should we. As creatives, we are as big as our radiant body allows. "It's not the life that matters, it's the courage that you bring to it." - Yogi Bhajan

7. Industriousness - a hardworking bird, a falcon gets the job done! A creative person with a strong radiant body has the "keep up spirit" and takes a project from conception to delivery.

8. Nobility - One look at a falcon flying and you know it commands the sky. The same is said about any person who has a strong radiant body; they possess noble presence and charisma to attract the help they need. A creative person not only needs an audience, but the strength to hold it; and they can attain both by strengthening their radiant body.

WHAT ARE YOU GRATEFUL FOR?

If yoga is connection between the finite us and the infinite us and as we've learned, both creativity and prosperity are manifestations of this connection, I think it's safe to say that Prosperity and Creativity cannot exist without gratitude.

"The attitude of gratitude is yoga. Ingratitude is "un-yoga," like "un-cola." Where gratitude is, there is yoga. Where there is ingratitude, yoga is gone. That mind which does not live in gratitude is just like a junkyard. There are great cars there, but they don't work; they are useless, because they are junk. What are you without gratitude?"

Gratitude is a wonderful thing. You could say that Creative Living is byproduct of an attitude of gratitude. And basically all the creativity and the prosperity of the Universe comes to you when you turn on the switch of gratitude. When you start to look at the pure magic and wonder of every single moment and start to appreciate everyone and everything around you, a portal opens up that is inexplicable. Every single experience you have is a learning moment whether it be good or bad; this is the opportunity to really put your gratitude to the test.

"Gratitude opens the door to ... the power, the wisdom, the creativity of the universe." - Deepak Chopra

Living in anxiety, fear, and doubt close up the flow of prosperity, (as well as the flow of creativity, healing and love) but living in gratitude opens it all up. Gratitude engenders optimism and grace and everything flows smoothly. Creative problem solving increases as you trust in your ability to imagine solutions. Seeing possibility where there was none is a result of gratitude. And since creatives and artists' lives depend on making something out of nothing, you can see how gratitude has a direct effect on creativity. Deepak Chopra also said that the best use of imagination is creativity and the worst use of imagination is anxiety. Write THAT one down!

So, if living in gratitude is new to you, you can start right now by saying "thank you". That really is the start. There are so many people in your world that are doing things for you, whether you realize it or not, and if you have the opportunity, saying "thank you" to them can make a huge difference…for you as well as for them. I am sure that there are conveniences you live with, natural beauty, passing time, a comfortable bed, promoting daily practices, delicious food, etc. that you take for granted. What if you actually gave thanks for these things in your life?

You have certain talents or abilities that have shaped who you are; talents and abilities that have allowed you certain privileges, opportunities, and fulfillment. Have you ever given thanks for those?

Appreciation and gratitude are big heart openers. And talking about heart openers, gratitude is essential when facing a crises. Your creative powers come forth to expand your world view -opening your heart and your intuition so that you can see solutions and opportunities. Gratitude also brings about compassion, the result of an open heart.

"Now there are many, many people in the world, but relatively few with whom we interact, and even fewer who cause us problems. So when you come across such a chance for practicing patience and tolerance, you should treat it with gratitude. It is rare. Just as having unexpectedly found a treasure in your own house, you should be happy and grateful toward your enemy for providing you that precious opportunity. Because if you are ever to be successful in your practice of patience and tolerance, which are critical factors in counteracting negative emotions, it is due to your own efforts and also the opportunity provided by your enemy."

~ Dalai Lama XIV ~

"Prosperity doesn't mean that you will have wealth, health and happiness. The best way to explain prosperity is to say it is like when a rosebud flowers and opens up, and it shares its fragrance. That's the moment, which lasts a few days, when a rose flower is prosperous. When a man or woman is prosperous, it is the fragrance of security, grace, depth, character, and truthfulness that a person can share. Like a candle emits light, a human emits prosperity."

Yogi Bhajan

CULTIVATING GRATITUDE

Listing - When I was a teenager, and I would feel sad or emotionally distraught, my father used to tell me to grab and pencil and a sheet of paper and make a list of what I was grateful for. It was a revelation to me at the time that you could write down a few things you were grateful for and the feeling of misery would vanish. Well, I can tell you that fifty years later that it still works. In fact, it is one of the most effective prosperity practices and one of the best ways to cultivate gratitude on a daily basis. Getting into the habit of acknowledging what you are grateful for is way to change the channel of your mind. *"Appreciation is an art and a lifestyle and a source of happiness and fulfillment. It's called gratitude—an attitude of gratitude."- Yogi Bhajan*

Clearing - Another really effective tool for cultivating prosperity and gratitude is getting rid of things that you don't use or need; this clears the path for prosperity and gratitude. A house of clutter leaves no room for growth. Just like a plant in a pot, once you reach the limit, you won't grow any more. And holding on to things is a reflection of holding on to old emotions. You don't have to throw everything away, you can donate or give things away. And since holding on to things and emotions is the antithesis of being in the flow, de-cluttering will remove blockages; creating movement in your life on many levels.

One thing, is that it gives you a deep appreciation for what you have and what pleasure they have given you. And if you give things away, you can appreciate how they can benefit others. The act of clearing creates a vacuum which initiates the flow of prosperity. When you make art and it leaves your hands, you are creating a similar flow. Living with less "stuff" is always a good practice. Less, waste, less clutter and chaos, and more room for expansion and appreciating the "little things" in life.

"Got no check books, got no banks - Still I'd like to express my thanks – I got the sun in the mornin' and the moon at night." - Irving Berlin, composer

Giving Thanks - And don't forget to say "thank you"….just these two words alone can start to change your relationship with prosperity. Yogi Bhajan said that he thought life means nothing but to give thanks.

"That's the purpose of life. There is no reason for narrowness and shallowness, for complaints ...but there is every reason for compliments and thanks."

If you started appreciating and stopped finding fault…yes, even with yourself, mountains will move. Opportunities will appear because you made room for them. Your whole view of the world will change. That shift into appreciation is a shift into finding art in your everyday world. It is the KEY that opens you to Creative Living.

"The Three Laws of Prosperity:

Be kind to everyone.

Speak not ill of others.

Speak not ill of yourself"

Yogi Bhajan

ART OF PROSPERITY HIGHLIGHTS

1. Prosperity is NOT just about the acquisition of riches. It's not a state of affairs, it's a state of mind.

2. Prosperity, like creativity, is an energy flow. It's easy to access but it takes a little effort to maintain.

3. Opportunity is just another form of prosperity. And when either prosperity or opportunity comes, if often doesn't come the way you've imagined it would.

4. Prosperity is like when a rosebud flowers and opens up, and shares its fragrance.

5. Living in anxiety, fear, and doubt close up the flow of prosperity.

6. Creativity is an expression of prosperity.

7. Keep your heart open, your mind clear and your intuition on point. That way, you won't be tempted by false opportunity. That way, you won't miss the good one when it comes.

8. The secret of prosperity is how you handle trauma and challenge in your life. Since we are growing and changing everyday, we have the chance and the know-how to improve ourselves. The better we handle things, the more prosperity, creativity, and love we can enjoy and share.

9. Appreciation and gratitude are the ignition system for experiencing prosperity and Creative Living in your life.

MEDITATION FOR PROSPERITY I

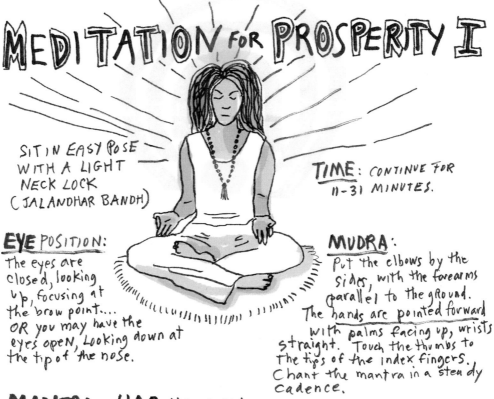

SIT IN EASY POSE
WITH A LIGHT
NECK LOCK
(JALANDHAR BANDH)

TIME: CONTINUE FOR
11-31 MINUTES.

EYE POSITION:
The eyes are
closed, looking
up, focusing at
the brow point....
OR you may have the
eyes open, Looking down at
the tip of the nose.

MUDRA:
Put the elbows by the
sides, with the forearms
parallel to the ground.
The hands are pointed forward
with palms facing up, wrists
straight. Touch the thumbs to
the tips of the index fingers.
Chant the mantra in a steady
cadence.

**MANTRA: HAR HA-RAY HA-REE
WHA-HAY GU-ROO**

This mantra uses the 3 qualities of HAR — SEED, FLOW AND COMPLETION
UNTO THE ECSTATIC INFINITY OF GOD

COMMENTS: This meditation provides guidance and the
way through any block. The future is clear, without
anxiety. Every cause has an impact and an orbit of
effect. This meditation allows you to use the neutral
mind to intuit all the expected and unexpected impacts
of the mental thoughts you feel NOW, or what were part of
the past. IF this part of you is unbalanced, people will
distance themselves socially out of subconscious fear of your
perception, bluntness and truth. When balanced, you
gain wisdom and self-guidance to hold in trust all that comes
to you. You are never swayed by abundance & hold closely to
the Path.

ART OF COMMUNITY

GROUP CONSCIOUSNESS IN ACTION

"As you grow older, you will discover that you have two hands, one for helping yourself, the other for helping others." - Maya Angelou

At the beginning of the book, I talked about the Universal Mind and what happens when each one of us merges into the vast every-one-of-us. This is proof positive of the power of community to take a limited ego-centric human being and embrace them into the limitless universal creative group consciousness.

The Sat Sangat is a spiritual group made up of people who gather to create something bigger than the sum of its parts. Whether you are already part of a spiritual, artistic, business, sports, political, or healing community etc. or looking to build one, there is power and potential in the group dynamic. By groups joining together to develop the body/mind/spirit machine, the effort one makes toward a desired goal is met.

"Exactly when we create a magnetic field by the tuning of the individual mind into one universal mind into such gathering we change the basis of our magnetic field as individuals. Thus we gain the constant purity of the mind. Such mind when seeks and seeks and seeks through sadhana and sat sangat. Now these are two words: sadhana and sat sangat. Sadhana means to purify oneself, sat sangat means company of the such who are seeking to purify.

Sat means truth, sangat means the company. Truthful
company, when the sadhana is done in the truthful
company the mind expands."

When you do sadhana, meditation, yoga, and chant mantras in community, the group aura of people coming together to meditate stimulates the meditative energy of all. This is the basic principle behind sat sangat; it is the highest reality that includes all those who come with grace and sincerity to merge their higher consciousness with the Universal Mind. Sometimes you might have a problem or challenge that you feel you can't take on alone and collective effort is required. Yogi Bhajan said:

"We have a collective strength in us,
hand in hand, in friendship, in the love,
and in the affection. Do not keep things
to yourself and say, 'I cannot.' There is
nothing you cannot do."

In community, you test out the theories hatched in isolation, you collaborate and share talents and skills, you get to practice what you preach and you pool your resources; be it financial, creative, philosophical or energetic. And in community, it is easier to affect change and make things happen.

One of the most powerful tools for social change and community transformation is a spiritual form of activism called Compassionate or Subtle Activism.

COMPASSIONATE ACTIVISM

Compassionate Activism refers to consciousness-based practices to create collective transformation. Global meditation, community events, and other large group consciousness raising gatherings are effective in everything from healing populations ravaged by natural disaster to supporting the peaceful resolution of an international conflict. Not intended as a replacement for overt forms of protest or action, Compassionate or Subtle Activism is an effective component of the peace, sustainability and social justice movements.

How does Compassionate Activism fit into the creativity model?

Because it involves self-realization merging with universal realization, transmuting ideas into actions, and the bulk of it's effect and purpose is creating impact. When we create focused intention and/or prayer on a particular group of individuals or an issue, this in itself has tremendous impact. By using mindfulness practices, meditation, and concentrated effort toward a cumulative goal, this is creative group consciousness in action.

If the same life force energy or prana is replacing our cells every seventy-two hours and is responsible for changing our cellular make-up as well as our inner mental landscape, then we - as the microcosm of the Universe - can use it to alter social structures and political landscapes.

In many creative situations (think writers' rooms, collaborative art projects, theatre, poetry groups, musical and dance productions, sports teams) there is a certain sensitivity that has to be developed. Yogi

Bhajan taught and counseled many sports teams and used Kundalini yoga technology to build team consciousness, to enhance performance and develop character.

A successful athlete (not unlike an artist, performer, or other creative) has a radiance or charisma that is the result of developing inner qualities like courage, selflessness, focus, stamina, and commitment. And in athletics, like in most team activities, developing sensitivity to the energy flow is an extra added resource. When our psycho-electro-magnetic bodies meld with the group aura, anything is possible.

"I ask every man who would seek peace to realize that peace doesn't come by protests and rallies. Peace comes by peaceful actions, and so long as those born of the mother will not learn to respect the woman, there shall not be any peace on this planet. The day the woman will not be exploited on this planet, there shall be peace on this Earth".

COMPASSIONATE ACTIVISM=SOCIALLY ENGAGED SPIRITUALITY

Compassionate Activism can take many forms; group meditations and prayer in person or through social media global events, ecstatic dance and movement practices such as Kundalini Yoga's Celestial Communication, shamanic journeying, mass chanting, and basically all forms of ritual performed in community. It is intended to work on the large scale; like large group chanting for rain to end a drought or subdue a fire, or meditating for peace in war-torn countries. Crowd-sourced prayers on social media are phenomenal machines of healing, even when focused on just one individual. The power and intention of group prayer on one person has the same impact as on many.

Compassionate Activism also uses methods that have their base in spiritual tradition and/or spiritual principles or any practice where the merging of consciousness is a major component. A phenomenon that often occurs when group meditations are organized near troubled or violent situations, like near war zones or high crime areas for example, is that violence and crime decreases.

The origin of Compassionate Activism is in yoga of all places!

In Vedic tradition, as in Kundalini Yoga, it is believed that certain mantras and sounds represent the vibration of natural elements and so form a blueprint for the functioning of the Universe. In large numbers, chanting mantras and reciting prayers are highly effective and powerful tools for change. The siddhis or superpowers that are attained by some advanced yogic practitioners demonstrate many "skills" that can be used to influence or change a situation crossing through time and space.

Imagine what good you could do if you possessed telepathic knowledge, or mastery over nature! Imagine if you got a group of individuals together who had these kinds of heightened abilities to change the material world. How could you use these skills to positively influence the minds of others, like political figures who don't have our best interest? With the collective power of community, a group meditating or chanting specific and intentional mantras, could broadcast and transmit seriously atomic healing and transformational energy around the globe. The following passage from the first chapter on the Universal Mind, is worth repeating here:

The Universal Mind is the vehicle for Compassionate Activism; a form of activism that is rooted in an underlying compassion for all beings. In "normal" activism there is an urge to dehumanize the opponent or to respond to violence with violence. Compassionate Activism is a philosophy of creating transformation on a Universal scale; beyond traditional binary paradigms, war logic, and typical social and political hierarchies. Compassionate Activism does not use domination or violence of any kind and strives to use methods like upgrading the thought waves and vibrations of large groups to influence cultural shifts. When large groups of people are active spiritually together, the force of the Universal Mind is unstoppable and unbeatable.

There is also something known as "Vedic defense" which was practiced by the followers of Maharishi Mahesh Yogi in the 1960's in order to change the vibrational frequency in discordant and violent communities. Building on one of Patanjali's sutras (avert the danger before it arises), the practitioners utilized various transcendental meditation techniques to bring social harmony in populations plagued by violence and chaos. Many studies were done of what was called the "Maharishi Effect"; in fact one was published in Yale University's Journal of Conflict Resolution. In addition to a decrease in war deaths and in the level of fighting, the number of car accidents, crime rates and other seemingly unrelated non-war occurrences dropped as well.

There were many such assemblies during the height of the Israel-Lebanon war in 1983. Have you ever heard of the "Big Ben Minute"? This involved the daily practice of one minute of silence during the chiming of Big Ben on BBC right before the 9pm news. Millions of people participated because this action provided moral and spiritual support for the Allied war effort in World War II.

Linking more than 1,000 meditation gatherings in 59 countries, the "Be the Peace" event (as part of the UN designated International Day of Peace) occurred on September 21, 2014 with the shared intention to support a shift to planetary peace. There was also a series of massive peace meditations in the 1990's organized by Dr. A.T. Ariyaratne in Sri Lanka to help facilitate a peaceful resolution to the.

Compassionate Activism is a highly sophisticated creative practice for transformation, renewal and a terrific tool for building like-minded socially conscious community. Activists and organizations are experimenting more and more with creative nonviolent approaches to instituting socio-political reform; the power of large collective meditation is being recognized as a viable tool for transformation as well as an accepted form of socially engaged art practice.

WHO ARE WE IF WE CAN'T EMBRACE OTHERS?

"We cannot seek achievement for ourselves and forget about progress and prosperity for our community... Our ambitions must be broad enough to include the aspirations and needs of others, for their sakes and for our own". - Cesar Chavez, activist

One of many wonderful things to come out of the Aquarian Age is the easy access to information sharing via the internet. The interrelatedness of all beings on the planet is enhanced by the ability to engage in group video chats, texting, emailing, messaging, sharing platforms and so on. A group of people living in different parts of the world can come together to meditate, have conversations, and work together all at the same time. This kind of consciousness sharing has created a "new-age Buddha" born of collective spiritual practice. Buddhist monk Thich Nhat Hanh's famous 2008 comment applies even more so now:

"Twenty-five hundred years ago, Shakyamuni Buddha proclaimed that the next Buddha will be named Maitreya, the "Buddha of Love." I think Maitreya Buddha may be a community and not just an individual. A good community is needed to help us resist the unwholesome ways of our time. Mindful living protects us and helps us go in the direction of peace. With the support of friends in the practice, peace has a chance."

When I was coming up as a young painter in the 1970's and 80's, there was no internet or Instagram accounts. If you wanted people to see your work, you had to invite them over to your place or your studio. Back then we all took slides of our work, put them in those clear plastic slide sheets and delivered them to gallery owners and whomever else we wanted to take notice. A lot of us put on our own, what would be later called, "pop-up shows" in warehouses, basements, bars, and each other's apartments.

Bach then, I was part of a collective group of New York artists who met regularly in the basement of a Lower East Side Polish church. Club 57, as it was called, was artist-run and it hosted events, art shows and performance based get-togethers. There were movie nights, musical theatre shows, Ladies' Wrestling, and just about any and everything else you could imagine. We went on excursions and field trips, put on talent shows, and threw down a good time for one another. I had the honor of putting on the first one-person painting exhibition which I called The Art Shebang. Forty years later, in 2017, the Museum of Modern Art in New York decided that the creativity that came out of Club 57 was essentially a movement and honored the members of Club 57 with a block-buster interdisciplinary exhibition. With everything from visual and media arts to installation and performance, Club 57 Film, Performance, and Art in the East Village, 1978 - 1983 was a hugely successful museum show that proved that even the most "innocent" and "unofficial" creative community has significant power and longevity.

Here I am at the opening with three of my Rhode Island School of Design college besties - class of 1976 - who came from near and far to support and applaud the success of the show.

Other art movements in history had their start in organized get-togethers or group activities where they would share newfound ideas, discuss radical concepts and use group get-togethers as laboratories for social change and creative experimentation. In this way, Surrealism which originated about one hundred years ago and was interested in the release of free-form creativity coming through the subconscious mind, were not that much different than the nurturing of unbridled creativity at Club 57.

Surrealism started out as a literary movement in the late 1910's and early 20's with exercises in automatic writing; they believed that it released the untapped imagination of the private world of the mind. It was officially "birthed" with the publication of the Manifesto of Surrealism by the poet and critic André Breton and eventually became a philosophical, political and art movement that used the then popular Freudian method of free association. Brainstorming as a group, they produced work that was unexpected and fresh in an art world dominated by tradition and the onset of War.

Why am I bringing up examples of the power of group consciousness around art - which includes the Feminist Movement, Abstract Expressionism, Social Practice and so on? Because busting loose of limited societal belief structures is their motivation. That is their driving force. One of the most powerful uses of community, is to use the Law of Creativity in a group dynamic.

CONCEIVING, FLOURISHING AND DELIVERING can be a high impact situation when a group of creatives decides to collaborate or co-create.

Dada was another "anti-art" movement that emerged at this time (1914-18) and like many other creative activists, were making art in response to the degradation of society; in particular, corrupt politics and repressive social values. They believed that conformity had to be questioned by challenging conventional ideas of art, culture and rational thought. The artists and poets who aligned themselves with the Dadaist philosophy and aesthetic (which was basically a non-aesthetic and secondary to the ideas conveyed) started out in Zurich and eventually grew into a widening international collective. This planted the seed for Conceptual Art and the performative work of the Social Practice movement.

In 1916 Hugo Ball, one of the founders of the Dada movement, described his poetry as an effort to "return to the innermost alchemy of the word". His comments on the personal rhythmic expression of his sound poems makes me think about the chapter on the Art of Healing:

"I don't want words that other people have invented... I want my own stuff, my own rhythm, and vowels and consonants too, matching the rhythm and all my own. If this pulsation is seven yards long, I want words that are seven yards long."

I think all this is testimony to the power of the Universal Mind; that community could be built and sustained without the technological advancements we have today. Artists and creative thinkers built strong international communities through an investment in non-digital social interaction - person to person, through writing and conversation - the principle of sat sangat works in creative circles, too!

Most "new" art movements come out of a reaction to something stale or unchanging and in that way, they are based on spiritual principles of transformation and keeping the flow of energy moving. When people of like mind come together to practice, throw ideas across the table, and share experiences, the group aura expands and this stimulates the creative capacity of all.

So it was therefore a revelation to me when my daughter, also an artist, started posting her artwork on a social media art site and she accumulated a rather supportive and large following in a relatively short amount of time. Social Media has created a vivacious on-line arts community that has forged both professional and personal relationships never before possible. Thousands of artists could join a platform and share work, ideas, opportunities and projects. These kinds of on-line communities can be found in political, social, cultural, religious, spiritual, and creative sectors as well.

The only problem is that contemporary society - and the powers that be - have evolved toward curating groups based on buying habits and commodification potential. In this way it pulls us further and further away from making our own choices and real person-to-person interactions. THAT'S why we have to stay aware of our human potential at all costs. That's why we have to continue to join together with our people, our sangat, our community.

Now more than ever, we have to rebuild social and professional relationships through spiritual and creative effort; creating group events, parties, get-togethers, self-initiated art shows and creative festivals, poetry readings, panels, meals, workshops and so on.

Besides on-line and "real" yoga offerings, The RA MA Institute of Yogic Science and Technology in Venice, CA (as well as a community center in South Los Angeles, and studios in Mallorca, Spain and the Lower East Side of New York) is doing that right now by hosting a plethora of community-based activities using Kundalini Yoga technology at its core. Activities such as study groups, gathering opportunities, spiritually-based *foreign travel, festivals and all kinds of creative projects and social events can be found on their website and social media. Theirs is an analogue and digital community-based model that works.*

"The most courageous, and pious act of a human is to be with another human, because we are like stars in the sky, born at one time and space, to be ourselves. Everybody is our neighbor. All we have to do is say, "I am with you." When you start being one with everybody, then you are actually with God, because if you cannot see God in all, you cannot see God at all."

In other words, this is not a time to isolate and shut people out on our journey. We need each other to succeed in this world for all of us to be successful. We should be happy when good fortune falls on someone in our community. Chances are they have good fortune because they've considered the collective. That's why one should consider the difference between healthy competition and unhealthy competition. Remember, if we are here to create impact, we can have a more profound impact if we consider our community as our partner and not as our enemy.

HEALTHY VS. UNHEALTHY COMPETITION

In sports, it's a common practice to engender healthy competition. If you were a runner, a good example would be the advantage of pairing yourself off with someone who is slightly faster than you. Having a "rival" in a race can make you run significantly faster. This is true in every area; experiencing what is possible can inspire you to try harder, go further than your self-created mental limits, and thus improve your speed. If in the race, your "rival" blocks you or tries to inhibit your progress, that is unhealthy competition. We've all seen this in one way or another; on the job, in the family and in community where the dynamics of power come into play. It's funny how even in a creative or spiritual community, there can be so much unhealthy competition when the whole point of it all is to foster mindful living and support for each other's work.

In Kundalini Yoga, we talk about three qualities of the mind that exist in all of us; they are called gunas. We all have them and how we use them determines how we behave in any given situation and how we interact with one another. Living, working, and being in community will always test you; it's like a litmus test for your spiritual progress.

"Your gunas, your fundamental quality as a human being and psyche, are your own productivity. You choose with each action and thought the altitude of your mind and life. Everything that happens around you and to you is not your guna, your basic personality, or your basic quality. Regardless of your history of abuses or kindness, opportunity, or challenge, it is

within you to direct your mind. You can be a saint; you can be a human; or you can be a demon."

Each and every one of us is made up of the three gunas. It's your choice whether you act impulsively as an animal, emotionally as a human, or as infinite as an angel.

When you ignore your sensitivity, you are acting like an animal acts; living by impulse and necessity. You may notice at times that you might be impulsive, reactive and territorial; this is the way an animal acts. Yogi Bhajan said *"If hungry, he has to eat. If horny, he has to mate. If threatened, he has to run or kill. The impulse is so strong it acts as a unifying force for the psyche of the animal. As a human, when you act as an animal, you are direct, focused, and robotic—ruled by habit and impulse."* People who practice unhealthy competition are running the animal guna (tamasic) program.

A normal earthling or human is run by feelings, thoughts and emotions. It's hard to maintain your clarity when you are confused by whether or not you should do something, or how you should feel and even confused about who it is that you are! Yogi Bhajan said that the more dependent you are on your feelings and emotions, the more mentally corrupt you become. If you get confused about who you are and lose your footing and humility in the process, chances are you would be practicing unhealthy competition; running wild with your feelings and emotions and all those mental intrigues that go with it.

This is called the ragisic guna.

But when you are acting in everyone's best interest, that is the way of an angel (sattvic guna). You are compassionate, elevated and kind; you are  true to your word. Everything you do is to promote peace and compassion. You have no ulterior motives, you are direct and you're pure. Yogi Bhajan said *"you can listen and act in the Will of God and the reality of your soul."*

An angel would practice healthy competition because they would always consider the greater good. They would allow community members to do what they needed to do and give them the space to do it well. Opportunities and possibilities that come to a community are for everyone.

The person who is running the animal guna program loves the heat of unhealthy competition and expects someone to win at the expense of someone losing. A "human" might get some emotional or dramatic payback from pitting themselves (or others) against each other.

A community cannot thrive with unhealthy competition in this way; it's triumph is dependent on collaboration and sharing and the pooling of resources. In the first chapter, I wrote that the ego was the only enemy of the The Universal Mind and that when we relate to the Universal Mind, we relate to the highest and most divine part of ourselves; the soul.

The sattvic guna brings out your intuitive nature, your creativity, and who you "really" are. A community of souls practicing Creative Living would be an incubator for compassionate work, creative ways to solve problems and to build prosperity among its members. A community of jealous ego-driven creatives is a recipe for disaster! The ego, which stands in the way of our being our most angelic selves, must be tamed and controlled by the mind…otherwise everything falls apart.

I am on a lonely road and I am traveling

Looking for the key to set me free.

Oh the jealousy, the greed is the unraveling

It's the unraveling

and it undoes all the joy that could be.

- Joni Mitchell, All I Want, 1970

Yogi Bhajan gave us a great lesson on how to keep things elevated. He said,

"The rule of life is very simple: each day increase the angel in you and decrease the animal in you."

The thing is…that the gunas create attachment and therefore bind us to the ego. While the yogi's goal is to cultivate *sattva* or their angelic nature, their ultimate goal is to transcend the mis-identification of the self with the gunas… and to be unattached to the duality of life. In other words, to be a person who is not affected by the pairs of opposites.

"When one rises above the three gunas that originate in the body; one is freed from birth, old age, disease, and death; and attains enlightenment"

- Bhagavad Gita

LISTENING - A POWERFUL COMMUNITY BUILDING SKILL

In any community be it spiritual, creative, business, scientific political, social, etc…there is a lot of time spent negotiating complex issues and ideas. Remember, an idea is something that comes from somewhere else, so if you are feeling proprietary ownership around "your" ideas, you can just leave that attitude at the door.

Artists and creatives are increasingly being invited into boardrooms and laboratories to bring in fresh blood and a new perspective. For example, I know of many residencies available to artists that provide opportunities for collaboration with members of the scientific community; a great idea for hatching new schemes for creative engagement with the public. Cross-disciplinary learning is now fairly common; math or science classes team up with art classes to bring together disparate forms of problem solving and project building.

All this is to say that creatives are not just making art in studios or for gallery viewing, performing on stage, or even "object making" as we know it. Performances can happen anywhere, they can be scripted or non scripted and can involve the audience in the act. Sometimes the "art" is a group engagement that might include the making of things... but the ownership is shared.

In a few chapters back where I discussed the "life-like art" of Alan Kaprow and the "Dharma art" of Chögyam Trungpa, it is clear that **Living is Art** and should be at this point in time, considered as such. "Community Based Learning" or Social Practice is now a verifiable and certifiable subject matter taught in elementary schools and institutions of higher learning.

This particular topic is of special interest to me because at sixty, I went back to school to get my Master of Fine Arts in Social Practice (then called Public Practice) at the Otis College of Art and Design in Los Angeles. Going to graduate school to get my advanced degree in Social Practice encouraged me to meld my artistic and spiritual identities; teaching Kundalini Yoga was as much as an art practice for me as a spiritual one.

The idea that community can be built on the yogic concept of sunni-ai or deep listening was a mind-blowing revelation. And it was during my time there and the writing of my thesis that I experienced the profound confluence and non-duality of the creative and the spiritual.

Social Practice embraces the idea that the audience or community is a collaborator in the work. Teaching, which is a group activity or engagement, is to some, a performative type of social practice that in academia is called "pedagogy". A big part of social practice occurs through conversation and relational skills often involving research, group dynamics, engendering trust, risk, self-reflection and facilitation. Holding workshops, panels, and discussions are commonplace in Social Practice or Community Based Learning circles...as well as the sharing of meals. When a group of social practice artists get together, you can bet your bottom dollar there'll be food involved. Deep listening is something that is essential in any meaningful spiritual or creative work that one does..as well as for conscious conversational communication.

Sharing, storytelling, recording, and transcribing the voice is a deep dive into a listening practice as well as listening to recorded ambient environments and musical sounds. In normal life, people generally tune out what is going on sonically around them but they really tune out when in conversation with each other. It's as if we have all but forgotten how to be attentive. It seems how to listen deeply has got to be re-learned. The greatest tool for learning how to listen is meditation.

Meditation is a technique for fixing the mind and attaining a state of consciousness that is different from our normal waking state. What one usually experiences in meditation is a heightened sense of connection and awareness of the world around us. Meditation is not religious or dogmatic. It is an important part of many spiritual disciplines. It is a way of concentrating the mind on a particular object, subject or action that brings about a state of openness in which fruitful input can be received.

In many spiritual disciplines, there is a focus on silence and stilling the moving mind and in others, on repetition of mantra and/or movement.

Kundalini Yoga uses both approaches. Art-making involves both of these practices and in many cases, the art practice becomes a meditation in itself. I think it's safe to say that paying attention or listening is a very essential component of almost all spiritual and artistic disciplines.

DEEP LISTENING AND SUNNI-AI

In 2016 we lost the veteran experimental composer, musician and performance artist Pauline Oliveros. She was widely recognized as a pioneer in contemporary music as a performer, composer, activist and educator. Always on the cutting edge of experimental music and sound making, she developed her *"Deep Listening Project"* as a full-blown evolving meditative practice that informed all of her compositional and socially engaged projects.

She had a long history of involvement with the electronic music scene both as a performer/composer and an educator. In 1967 she taught a hands-on course, The Nature of Music in which every student was expected to compose and improvise despite a lack of musical training. This inspired her Sonic Meditations, a body of work that could be done without musical training. The Sonic Meditations are ways of listening and responding that became the basis of her life's work Deep Listening.

Oliveros, when speaking about the meditative process of tuning into her environment explains,

"…so the music just comes out of that emptiness. I am able to clear my mind. I begin, with (what I think of as) deep listening; which is a very complete kind of receiving of what is. Whether its right next to me or is out in the audience or beyond the space that I'm in."

In 1981, Oliveros moved to upstate New York and in addition to her musical pursuits, studied many spiritual disciplines including Tibetan and Zen Buddhism, Yoga and meditation, and Tai Chi Chuan; all from accomplished teachers and masters. It was in 1991 and in the following ten years that Oliveros committed to her Deep Listening retreats at the Rose Mountain Retreat Center in Las Vegas, New Mexico where she developed the program and practices that appear in her famous workbook, *Deep Listening: A Composer's Sound Practice* (2005).

An engaged and dynamic artist, author, composer, performer, and humanitarian until the very end, she appeared at the Whitney Biennial in 2014 and presented her Deep Listening Room, a video and sound installation that was based on her life-long theory that attentive listening is a practice of expanded consciousness. The Deep Listening Room exemplifies the essential nature of her work; an art practice that acts as a meditative/spiritual tool for creativity and humanity building.

Yogi Bhajan often spoke about the the art of deep listening which was called sunni-ai in the yogic tradition. It means tuning into the sounds and subtlety that exist below the surface and hearing them; tuning into every and all sounds at the same time.

He described it as intuition applied to listening. It can be practiced all the time; when we are quiet and still or when we are speaking. It is a heightened state of awareness and applied consciousness that can change the way you navigate your world.

"The yogis say that in the yogic science, all of the knowledge in the universe is contained in your own sound. If I listen to my sound deeply enough, I can receive all the knowledge of the universe. In fact, my sound is more powerful than the anybody else's sound (to me.) Hearing my own current, to me, is going to be more powerful than hearing someone else's sound current. Sunn-ai means listening. It's that deep, deep, deep listening, so that you start to hear the unheard, see the unseen and know the unknown. It's the third eye."

- Gurujas, White Sun, 2017, LA YOGA Interview

Every time we utter a word, we are creating our world and everything we hear connects us to that world. Have you noticed that when people listen to us we automatically feel more connected to them? Listening carefully, you can read and feel all the unspoken cues. In fact, when people talk to each other, they are getting more from the cues than from the words. Yogi Bhajan said that an ordinary human being with a normal life only listens to six percent of a total conversation! This is why Deep Listening is so important in building community…otherwise no one knows what the heck anyone is talking about !

"Actually, today I want to tell you one of the greatest secrets: man is born as an animal to listen. This is one secret which, if you will never learn, you will never have the essence of life. It is man's basic quality: a being who listens."

The sound current is such a big part of yogic technology, that the better you can learn to deeply listen, the more depth and substance your life will have. How you project, what impact you have, how you translate thought forms into ideas, what kinds of information you "get" from the Universal Mind..all this is in your listening. The better you listen, the more creative your life will become. **Deep listening gives you real creative power.**

HEALING/BUILDING COMMUNITY WITH MUSIC AND SOUND

Back in the 1980's there was a flurry of consciousness and fund-raising musical concerts created to build awareness and compassion and accumulate revenue for underserved populations. You may have heard of England's "Band-Aid" and the USA's "We Are the World" (which came after); both targeted Africa's horrendous living conditions and life-threatening famine. The collaborative of high profile diverse musicians called USA for Africa that performed in the "We Are the World" events, spawned other iterations; one of which, for example, was to help Haiti after the earthquake of 2010, many years later and other such humanitarian fund-raising concerts like Farm-Aid.

I am not suggesting that you should start listening to "We Are the World", but you should at least know about it. It has been recognized as a politically important song, which brought a much needed focus on famine in Africa which had previously been ignored. Stephen Holden from the

New York Times suggested that since then, efforts had been made to use popular music to address humanitarian concerns. "We Are the World", along with Live Aid, Farm Aid and recently Kirtan Aid in 2017 showed that rock and popular music could become more than just entertainment and spiritual music could be used to fund-raise.

While these kinds of fund-raising concerts are highly commercial enterprises, they did manage to raise millions for famine relief and other social and political issues through the sale of recordings, product, and concert tickets. If you consider the message and the intention behind it, I suppose you could say that these concerts were a form of Compassionate Fundraising as well as Compassionate Activism. "We are the World", no matter what you may have thought ..or think of it today, delivered a very basic spiritual law and an uplifting community message; in order to heal the world and the people in it, we have to come together as one and show how much we care for each other.

"If you are at all serious you have to find out whether human beings, that is you and I, can bring about a total revolution in ourselves psychologically. When you change not at a superficial level but fundamentally, you affect consciousness, because you are the world and the world is you." - Krishnamurti

While we're on the subject of concerts, even rock concert-goers experience the sensation of oneness as they become an ocean of vibration flowing together in unison. This feeling grows and expands which creates a blissful, ecstatic state. If you go to a club or concert, you might call it a "vibe", but changes do most certainly occur on the physical, emotional and spiritual levels.

In the yogic world or any other community where meditation is a big part, one experiences the loss of self as an exhilarating feeling; the loss of ego being the root cause. Yes, it's totally possible to experience the loss of ego and melding into Universal Consciousness even at a rock concert.

Music just makes us feel better about things. I remember as a small child having relationships with certain pieces of music that would uplift me; I knew that music had that power. The Bach Brandenberg Concertos were a treasure trove of exhilarating musical passages that could move me into better emotional places where I felt comforted and elated. In Kundalini Yoga we say that your thoughts have a certain location that you can change if you wish. I knew that I could do that at six years old because the music told me so.

Another way to put it is, if you don't like the music, change the station. Music can transform your moods and even without formal training, can give you increased focus, a tendency to be more socially interactive, reduce stress levels and engender empathy. Both music and meditation have this effect.

Music has been used to build community and keep it together, raise consciousness and keep it lifted, relieve pain, heal, and facilitate social justice since the beginning of time. It's a part of all authentic spiritual traditions and has been used in ritual to focus the mind and explore deeper truths. Think of the up-swirling trance-state of chanting mantras or the heart opening and soul ignition that goes on when you are caught in the fever of a gospel choir in full swing.

Plato wrote that the cosmos was constructed according to musical proportions and intervals, Pythagoras called the celestial sounds "Music of the Spheres" and believed that we were connected to it through our inner ears since birth. The Sufis call it Saute Surmad or the tone that fills the cosmos, The Bible refers to it as "the Word", Sikhs call it Anahat which means the un-struck melody. In fact, in most esoteric spiritual traditions, it is taught that the cosmic sound of God is everywhere and can be explored and experienced in deep meditation.

The very word, Universe means One Sound or Song.

The dynamic impact of creative energy that was sent out as a sound vibration from the Supreme Force into the abyss at the dawn of creation is still being sent out as vibrational frequencies and waves. Scientists call it "Cosmic radiation" - residue from the big bang. The rhythm of the sound current forms every living thing, holds our structure in balance and directs our consciousness. Almost everything is formed, shaped and affected by the waves of sound which you can see in the patterns in nature in radial and spiral formations. The universe is made of sound. Everything is vibrating at their own particular frequencies, including us. Rocks have a slow frequency whereas light frequencies move fast through the space vacuum.

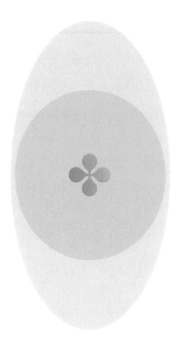

Virtually every civilization in the world has had some type of creation myth involving sound; the celestial sound being the seed from which all else sprung forth. Mastering the Sound Current as a generator of creative community is a major part of Kundalini Yoga.

USING SOUND TO GENERATE CREATIVE COMMUNITY

"When we chant a mantra, if the rhythm is right, and the concentration and surrender to its pulse is practiced, then the central nervous system vibrates it, and we can listen and absorb the sound. The mantra is attuned to the Infinite and when the Infinite resounds in us we achieve excellence. As Yogi Bhajan says: 'The science of reality is to find the sound and to resound in that sound. Then the soul shall excel and God shall dwell within you.' Anahat is that state in which the nervous system vibrates the mantra without conscious effort; we vibrate in harmony with the psyche of the universe, beyond anything we could create from our finite self or ego." - Harijiwan Khalsa

Naturally, we need to start vibrating with ourselves. It is recommended that you sleep to mantras, listen to them during the day, mentally chant mantra as you go about your business. This may seem like s a relatively "passive" method but it's effective and very powerful. I play mantras when I sleep and I have mantras playing 24/7 in my home. I listen to mantras in my car, when I am working, and if I need to shift energy for any variety of reasons. There are times when a space you occupy needs clearing and a mantra will do that for you. Whenever students ask how best they can improve a situation, I always recommend mantra.

The sound current is the basis of all life; it connects you to your pure self and to Universal Consciousness. You can listen to mantra, chant them mentally or in a whisper, or you can chant them out loud. Make a recording of yourself chanting a mantra; play it while you sleep or play it nonstop in your home. When you fall in love with our own sound current, then you'll have the world in the palm of your hand.

"The one who falls in love with ones own sound current can control all the currents vibration, creative, non-creative, destructive, non-destructive balancing, imbalancing, in polarity and all of neutralization of the planet, its space, and beyond space to the essence of creativity into the essence of oneself. That is God."

Music has been a big part of Kundalini Yoga since the late 1960's when Yogi Bhajan arrived in the United States. Many of his students were musically inclined and so the early years literally exploded with recordings of mantras, live kirtan and meditations as many latent talents were unleashed through the yoga practice. Early students often worked directly with Yogi Bhajan to bring his poems and mantras to life.

Music and mantra was, and still is, a big part of the Kundalini Yoga experience as you might find if you go to classes. Why? Because of it's potential to create a desirable high frequency vibratory field and create rhythmic patterns. We all know how powerful the sound current is and how music can create altered states of consciousness so one must be care of what you let into your system…especially when you are open and vulnerable to energies.

"I want you to judge music at what center comes what. You should receive it, you should drink it and get in

you, then you will know what music can do. Through
which hole it enters you."

Therefore, in Kundalini yoga classes, or when practicing on your
own, it is not recommended to play *other* kinds of music. Of
course, you can enjoy any kind of music you want anywhere,
anytime..but just not while doing Kundalini Yoga. When asked
why, Yogi Bhajan explained that because the practice
creates calm inner energy, you wouldn't want to provoke
the commotional outer energies that "other" kinds of music
might activate.

As in the old days, modern Kundalini yogic practitioners are
inspired to create new mantric music of their own. In order
to "get it right", one has to create a sound current that has
the caliber and frequency to enter the mind, body and
spirit of the listener, to chant correctly pronounced
mantras in the proper rhythm, and deliver it with a pure
devotional attitude…all of which is quite a creative feat.

"The power of the song and the smile is the most
divine power a human can enjoy. Make the songs, make
the music. Reach every heart. Open up every heart.
Bring to the consciousness of the people the message
of tranquility, grace, nobility, and peace. As long as
the people can smile and they can sing their songs, no
nation can be destroyed."

Which brings me to White Sun...

White Sun is an American musical group that was formed in Los Angeles and consists of Gurujas Khalsa (singer/songwriter), Adam Berry (producer/instrumentalist) and Harijiwan Khalsa (founder/ percussionist). White Sun collaborates with some of the greatest musical talents in the world and is produced by member Adam Berry who has a highly decorated musical career of his own. In addition to winning a Grammy for Best New Age Album in 2017, White Sun's music has been used in studies at UCLA's Neuropsychiatric Hospital and has been featured in the Psychiatric Times. White Sun is also on the course syllabus for USC classes where it is used to study stress management among students. Under Harijiwan's direction, White Sun creates complex energetic soundscapes which are framed inside highly sophisticated melodies and rhythms. When I listen to their music, I find that it can be quite cinematic and somatic.

When asked about the origin of the the name "White Sun", Gurujas replied in an interview for Hindustan Times:

"Harjiwan gave it this name - it has a profound meaning, for in all time, space and universe, it is the central sun. Harjiwan formed the band because he wanted to bring Gurbani mantras to a larger audience so that many more people could benefit from them. The sound of these mantras has changed so many lives."

White Sun creates music that is changing the planet as I write this. With each recitation and reverberation of mantra, more and more souls are becoming happier, healthier, and feeling more in control of their lives. Children say good-bye to night fears, grown-ups drop life-long debilitating habits, people wean themselves off of anxiety and pain medications, and stress levels are dropping dramatically. When YOU transform, the world transforms. The philosophy behind White Sun, which is to make things better for people and to make the world a more beautiful place, is behind every song they record.

It's the most subtle yet the most powerful form of compassionate activism there is!

If you are new to a Kundalini Yoga practice, or if you are interested in experiencing first-hand the transformational power of sound, I suggest you start here. Looking for this kind of music can be overwhelming because there is so much out there, but not so much of *this* quality. And when learning mantric technology, pronunciation is paramount. Gurujas is very masterful in this way.

Each member of the group is highly trained in the technology and deeper truths of the sound current. They understand and practice the potential of music to open doorways to the infinite, and in doing so, generate, nurture and deliver real transformational experiences. I've seen it in others and I've see it in myself. People who know nothing of yoga or spiritual music have been touched by the energy of the Gurbani mantras; all they have to do is hear it. As a teacher, I've seen communities grow around the positive effect it has on them.

From a 2016 BMI article, Gurujas and Adam talk mantras:

Gurujas: Mantras have a vibratory frequency that doesn't exist in other kinds of music, so there are all kinds of magical, mystical things that start to happen to people when they listen. Some of these mantras have been in existence for thousands of years, and they were designed to create a better feeling in the human being, to bring a more positive frequency to the planet. It's not about tradition or religion, it's about energy. It's about giving someone a way to feel better, right now, just by listening. And everything we do with the music of White Sun is to further project and expand that positive force of the mantra. Music is a very powerful force. One of the most effective ways to shift someone's energy is through music.

*Adam: Yes, exactly! And I base my entire scoring career on that concept. It's been shown in numerous experiments that different kinds of music create different psychological AND physiological states in the listener. But this just touches the surface. **Music is capable of opening up infinite spaces in the listener.***

Let's say you are an artist and you want to get into the Flow of your Creativity and you are not necessarily a yogic practitioner, or have knowledge of the meaning of the mantras. You can use recordings like the music of White Sun to access the Creative Flow; the mantras themselves have powers. At the beginning of the book, I talk about uplinking to the Universal Consciousness in order to download thought waves and turn them into ideas. There's a lot of information and cosmic creativity floating around out there just waiting to be picked up by your radar. You don't have to believe in anything in order to chant or listen to mantras. Anyone can use them. The mantras work because of the science of *Naad,* a balanced universal pattern of sounds.

"Senses and communication. All what that moves creates a vibration. And that is Naad. In the modern technology, in the depth of the ocean, from pure sound we can understand what kind of submarine is. Submarine is at the depth. And submarine can know what kind of ship is, ship can know what kind of submarine is. Same way, the big fish knows the small fish and small fish knows the big fish. As we move, our psyche knows our existence and our existence knows our psyche. That is all external at the larger situation but there is a communication - song of life - that is between the soul and the mind and from the mind of the being. But to overcome our mental strength to reach a point where we can excel in life, there are certain graduations. That is we create a sound which is understandable. Languages are different, but all that means is "understandable sound."

ART OF COMMUNITY HIGHLIGHTS

1. Joining together with others to develop the body/mind/spirit machine, the effort one makes toward a desired goal is met.

2. In community, you can test out theories hatched in isolation, collaborate and share talents and skills, you get to practice what you preach and pool your resources; it is easier to affect change and make things happen this way.

3. Compassionate Activism, whose origin is in yogic principles, uses group consciousness to affect change on a large scale.

4. *"We cannot seek achievement for ourselves and forget about progress and prosperity for our community... Our ambitions must be broad enough to include the aspirations and needs of others, for their sakes and for our own".* - Cesar Chavez

5. One of the most powerful uses of community is to use the Law of Creativity in a group dynamic. CONCEIVING, FLOURISHING AND DELIVERING can be a high impact situation when a group of creatives decides to collaborate or co-create.

6. There is a big difference between healthy competition and unhealthy competition; healthy competition is for the good of all whereas unhealthy competition is not.

7. *"The rule of life is very simple: each day increase the angel in you and decrease the animal in you."* - Yogi Bhajan

8. Deep listening gives you real creative power.

9. The yogis say that everything you need is in your own sound. When you fall in love with our own sound current, then you'll have the world in the palm of your hand.

10. Music and Sound are the most powerful form of Compassionate Activism there is.

11. Learn to master the Sound Current as a generator of Creative Community. When you change your relationship to sound, your projects, your relationships, your families, your community, in fact, the whole world - in one way or another - follows your lead.

12. Creative and dynamic ways of communicating builds community

13. Pay attention to what you say and how you say it. Pay attention to what others say and how they say it. Once you get on this level of acute awareness, you'll start to control what goes out and what comes in. This is a very important tool to have. How and where you deliver and how and where you receive are important skills to acquire in your Creative Living Experience.

MEDITATION TO KNOW THE FIELD

* THIS MEDITATION WAS TAUGHT BY YOGI BHAJAN IN VANCOUVER, B.C. to Canada's Olympic Swim Team IN 1973

THIS MEDITATION DEVELOPS A TASTE FOR THE EXPERIENCE OF EXPANDED AWARENESS. IT CREATES SENSITIVITY AND THE ABILITY TO EXTEND the AURA OUT TO LINK WITH THE WHOLE TEAM ENERGY. YOU WILL KNOW WHAT IS HAPPENING TO EVERYONE AT THE SAME TIME, AND SENSE WHERE THEY ARE, and SENSE WHAT THEY ARE ABOUT to DO. THE SENSING INCLUDES THOSE OPPOSING YOU, TOO. YOU WILL DEVELOP THE ABILITY TO SENSE THE ENERGY FLOW IN ANY SITUATION. FIRST DO A VIGOROUS YOGA SET WHICH INCLUDES PRANAYAM.... THEN PRACTICE THIS MEDITATION.

POSTURE: SIT IN EASY POSE WITH SPINE ERECT

EYES: EYELIDS ARE 1/10TH OPEN WITH EYES LOOKING DOWNWARDS. CONCENTRATE MENTALLY AT THE THIRD EYE POINT.

MUDRA: HANDS ARE IN GYAN MUDRA (THUMB AND INDEX FINGER TOUCHING)

FOCUS: KEEPING the SPINE STRAIGHT, BEGIN RELEASING all the tension from the spine OUTWARD. Let each segment of the spine Release and each area of the body RELAX.

TIME: CONTINUE FOR 22 minutes. It will take about 11 minutes to release your tension. IN the second cycle of 11 MINUTES, all your INTUITION CAPACITIES will be aroused.

BLUEPRINT FOR CREATIVITY

I bet you are wondering why I consider the Blueprint for Creativity to be the Eleventh Yogic Art.

Since a blueprint is a plan of something you intend to build and I am assuming that you are reading this book because you want to build a more vibrant, creative life for yourself, it seemed only natural to include it as such.

Coming up with a dynamic plan is always a good place to start in any creative undertaking. The whole point of this book is to get you thinking about how you might infuse more creativity into your daily life and how you might be able to use yogic technology to make your creative life better. Drawing up a Blueprint for Creativity will give you some structure around being more present and aware, more productive, more heart-centered and more courageous.

So here we are - yoga enthusiasts, serious practitioners and dabblers, people interested in boosting creativity or adding some additional creative juice in their lives, non-artists and non-yogis who are interested in turning things around, successful artists who want to have more control over their creative energy and production…maybe they'd like to learn how to avoid burnout, or those interested in exploring the ways in which spiritual practice and creative practice tap from the same energy stream.

Art teachers, academic teachers and yoga instructors can benefit from this technology as well - Kundalini yoga is extremely user-friendly, practical and it actually works.

I've been helping people give birth to their creative selves way before I even got into teaching about the yoga/creativity connection. Feeling confident about one's creative work and enjoying "play" are pleasures that most people have denied themselves as adults. Children are courageous when it comes to making things; they don't get wrapped up in self-judgment and what other people think of the expression of their creativity. That purity of intent and expression starts to muddy once they get exposed to evaluation and being compared to others in school. When young artists realize that their skills actually improve when they apply themselves and "work" at it, this is the biggest paradigm shift; how the virtue of self-discipline leads to self-mastery. You know, young people are either on board for the challenge or they are not.

"Every child is an artist. The problem is how to remain an artist once we grow up." - Pablo Picasso

Most people, whether they consider themselves artists or not, spend a big chunk of their adulthood trying to locate and return to the creative innocence they experienced as a child. This conscious awareness without aggression is what dharma artists and "living as art" practitioners have always aimed to embrace.

THE BASIC TENETS

Being an artist, educator and a yogi has given me some experience in navigating this creative terrain. Because of my hard-earned "navigational skills", and with the help of the Teachings of Yogi Bhajan, I am pretty sure that I can point you in the direction of some serious creative transformation.

Sustaining states of sublime creative insight and the limitless energy to act on on them is every artist's dream. Without having some sort of discipline to foster the creative spark and the energy to ignite it, you'll find projects hovering in limbo between the flourishing and delivery stages of creativity. Does that sound familiar? It should because so many projects out there never make it to the delivery stage because of fear of judgement, fear of failure, and fear of what might happen if the delivery of the project creates success. Yes… fear of being great can hold you up. It's a big juicy issue for a lot of creative people. The fear of success and the responsibilities that come with it can freeze you up if you don't have the nervous system strength and the bandwidth to handle it.

Many people get stuck in this place of pre-delivery and that is why having a blueprint of daily actions can effectively override your programmed tendencies of inertia and/or crippling fear. Having a daily practice will build your nervous system strength which in turn amps up your radiance; that's a given. But it also gives you confidence, clarity, intuition, ace communication skills, and the kind of aura that can handle the attention.

Being a creative person of course does not mean you have to be in the spotlight, it just means living life in a different way. Creative Living embraces the spectrum of "being" creative. For some of us, just learning how to experience a deeper appreciation for the life we have now, though simple as it may seem, can be a daunting task. It's not easy to be with "what is" when we have been instructed in Western culture to focus on "what isn't". The simple shift in perspective from "what isn't" to "what is" is, in itself a very profound spiritual teaching.

So here is how it works. You have to do some soul-searching. What do you hope to achieve in terms of stepping into YOUR version of Creative Living? How much time do you have to give to yourself for your practice? If you go over the chapters in this book, it will give you some guidance as to areas that might need some "attention" shall we say.

If, for example, you feel run down and over-extended you could revisit the chapter on Self-Care; that might give you some ideas as to how you could put together a daily practice that would focus on taking care of YOU. Self-Care Breath is short and sweet and the Rejuvenation Meditation is a profound practice for glandular system regeneration; anyone can do either of these two meditations… even sitting in a chair. The sub-chapter on Self-Care for Creatives is a list of what creative people need to pay attention to so that they stay healthy in body and mind.

There are some other tools I list at the end of this chapter which are targeted for those who want to jumpstart their creativity in a more traditional "artistic" manner. Both spiritual habits and creative habits, (after all, we are developing new habits) have to be practiced consistently over time. The basic Yogi Bhajan teaching on this is 40 days to break a habit, 90 days to establish a new habit, 120 days to confirm the new habit so that it is permanently established, and 1000 days will give you mastery of the habit. Think of the Blueprint for Creativity as a new chapter in your life and an opportunity for you to really get down to business.

Working with these principles will give you a solid foundation of what starts and stops the creative flow, how to maintain it once you're in the groove, and how to avoid sabotaging your creative self. My belief is that once we learn to manage our own creativity, we can inspire others - by our example - to do the same. That's why I believe that a Blueprint for Creativity has the seed potential to grow and expand for all; to inspire others to create courses, workshops, retreats, and community-based projects - all with the goal of becoming a hatchery for ideas, collaboration, relationship-building and group transformation.

Back in November of 1978 Yogi Bhajan said:

"Creativity is your essence, creativity is your projection and creativity is your comfort. Lack of creativity gives you anger, frustration and fear and it has a reaction. Whether you like God or you don't like God, whether you like Dharma or no Dharma, whether you like a yogi or no yogi... don't misunderstand that part. Whether you like yourself or not yourself, whether you have a good image of yourself or you don't have a good image of yourself that is a secondary issue. Fundamental issue is, do you flow or you don't. Do you flow and receive the experience of your own creativity or not?

CULTIVATE REVERENCE

First off, you need to cultivate what Yogi Bhajan called "reverence". What is reverence? It's a deep respect for someone or some thing. It comes from the latin word revereri which means to stand in awe of. Reverence blossoms with the opening of the heart.

What would happen if you started living each and every day in a state of deep appreciation? How would your life change if you brought awareness and consciousness to each and every act: sharpening a pencil, cleaning brushes, doing vocal scales, stretching before a run, making a cup of tea, opening the shades in the morning, peeling a potato, walking your dog, washing the dishes. These things that you and I may take for granted and perform mindlessly are basically karma yoga actions that have the potential to change your magnetic frequency. And just think....from that perspective, you could change the vibration of every thought and every action you perform. Every single person you encounter could be touched by this love force activated in you and then your life could be an expression of love, generosity and gratitude …instead of fear, attachment and resentment.

There are some actions (we might call them obligations) we feel we "have" to do, but if we feel reverence when we perform them - or at least aim to appreciate them for what they are - those very same actions have the potential to bring us much pleasure and creative joy.

"There's a very magical word called reverence. If I start to have reverence and I start to appreciate the sacredness, the uniqueness of the moment, of the situation, of the person, and I activate that as a flowing mental movement, reverence, that activates the Love force, and that will give me the power and elevation to move through whatever I need to move through." - Harijiwan

Creative Living is living as an inspired human being. In the Zen Buddhist tradition, it is referred to as dharma art or the art in everyday life and many artists have been inspired by this kind of thinking; in other words, less about product and more about process. When "making art" from this perspective, reverence itself becomes the creative act.

In the chapter on the Art of Impact, I discuss the creative awareness practices of a group of artists (who also happen to be or have been practicing Buddhists). The legendary composer and performer Meredith Monk spoke often about the parallels between dharma and making art.

"As the years go on, I realize more and more that there is no separation between the two: making art is a bodhisattva activity. The inner transformation and growth that results from dharma practice flow into the work, and the work in turn becomes an offering."

The OG conceptual artist Marcel Duchamp (who was not a card-carrying Buddhist) is credited for changing not only how we experience art, but how we experience life. He said: *"If you wish, my art would be that of living; each second, each breath is a work which is inscribed nowhere, which is neither visual nor cerebral. It's a sort of constant euphoria."*

Everyday actions done with appreciation and attention take on unprecedented power because according to Yogi Bhajan, reverence equals Infinity. The art of the meditative experience is available to everyone; all that is needed is slowing down and deepening one's breath. Even when we do this most basic and simple breathing exercise, we are activating the pituitary gland and waking up to the experience of heightened awareness and attention. As you allow more and more breath and prana into your lungs, your heart chakra melts open and suddenly everything is infused with the loving heart energy; the mundane becomes extraordinary as you shift into the consciousness of the heart.

And now a message from the 1955 musical Damn Yankees...

You gotta have heart ...miles and miles of heart...

Oh it's fine to be a genius of course, but keep that old horse before the cart...

First you've gotta have heart.

"Life has no meaning without reverence. If there is no reverence, there is no life. First of all reverence should be for yourself. Second, reverence for all the environments, thirdly all projections should be just with reverence. All achievements meant to give you reverence. If you cannot create reverence, the time will reverse on you; you will be victim of one thing or the other, there is nothing, it's just, it's just going through the pain. Don't misunderstand, doesn't matter how much you have, who you belong to and what you are talking about, life without reverence is just reverse tragedy of self. There's absolute cut and dry rule in it, either or."

-Yogi Bhajan

MEDITATION FOR THE BLOSSOMING OF THE SELF

OPENING FEEL "I. AM.THE INFINITY" UP.

* IN 40 DAYS, WITHOUT A ROSE NEAR YOU, YOU'LL BE ABLE TO smell it. JUST FEEL you are BLOSSOMING

MUDRA: Bend the elbows down by the sides, and bring the butts of the hands together so they are touching in front of the throat center. SPREAD the fingers apart. CUP the hands and fingers to slightly form a "FLOWER"

MOVEMENT: Keep the butts of the hands together the entire time and the hands up at the level of the throat center. Begin gently bringing the fingertips and thumb tips together to touch, and then gracefully begin opening them WIDE, as if a flower is blossoming OPEN continue opening and closing the "flower"

EYES: CLOSED   **TIME:** practiced 11 minutes

END: INHALE and RELAX

DEVELOP INTUITION

Reverence, an elevated state of consciousness, will open up our intuitive faculties. So the second thing we must develop and strengthen is our intuition.

Creativity and intuition have a beautiful synergistic relationship. Yogi Bhajan said that intuition is in everyone, but lies dormant in most people. If it is dormant, you are living from instinct, like an animal. The key to Creative Living is to develop the highest aspect of yourself, in other words your angelic nature, in order to raise your frequency and move through life consciously and with grace.

We create many habits during the course of our lifetime and then the habits create us. Hopefully at this point, you have some meditative practice that you do on a daily basis. If not, now is a as good a time as any to create the habit of meditation. One of the beautiful things about meditation is that it will make you intuitive and intuition can take care of a lot of life's problems.

One of those problems is living from impulse; a person who lives purely from impulse doesn't have a chance. A human being needs intuition to navigate the world, to see the big picture, to see the consequences of their actions, to know the way.

Artists thrive on intuition; it's a portal into realm of creativity. So if you create the habit of meditation, intuition will guide you and you will most likely have very little if any struggle in your artistic projects. Why is that? "Because you can only pre-organize with intuition; you cannot do it with thinking" Yogi Bhajan explained. *"Thinking only will bring your past into today, and those who live in the past have no future."*

Most creative projects involve organization; of ideas of course, but also of spacial relationships and the management of time and the talents of other people as well as materials, media and research. Without intuition, you could waste endless amounts of time heading in the wrong direction. If you use intuition, you could anticipate what you might face in the development of a new project; what might go right, what might go wrong. In either case, you are ready for it. You'll end of making more efficient choices, that's for sure!

`"Thinking is a waste of time: conflict, logic, argue, bring the feeling out, take the emotions out, see how you can cheat, how you can lie, how you can get by, how you can get over, how you can get under, how you can harpoon, how you can get it, how you can fish it out. The whole dirty game-it is garbage."`

We do not have the outer defense mechanisms of the animal kingdom; claws, sharp teeth, hooves, etc. so the only defense we have as humans is our intuitive capacity. Your sixth sense is a gift, but you have to open and activate it in order to enjoy it.

Intuition is knowing the unknown; imagine how life would be if you could live without fear, worry and doubt. Intuition removes them all! The only reason you have doubt in the first place is because you are not intuitive. The less intuition you have, the more in doubt you are. And the more in doubt you are, the more vulnerable you are to crisis and conflict because your position will not be secure… you'll be flipping and flopping on every issue…should I or shouldn't I? it is or it isn't? should I go or should I stay? and on and on. *You'll drive yourself nuts and everyone around you, too.*

You need to meditate in order to develop and fortify your intuition. The more you use it, the more you trust it and the stronger it gets.

"You know before you act. To know before it happens".

 I am sure you have met people in your life for who the first impression wasn't a favorable one. You felt it, but you decided to "override" your gut feeling. Maybe the person was cute or they could help your career or whatever tantalized you out of your good sixth sense. We have these intuitive "hits" all the time but maya is always testing you. You can save yourself a lot of trouble if you pay attention to what your intuition is telling you.

In creative projects, it's not that much different except we mostly get seduced by potential fame, acknowledgement or ego gratification; you might end up with projects and collaborations that cater to something other than your highest good. When you are not operating from intuition, you will most likely create all sorts of conflict and stress which ultimately numbs you out and robs your energy and the power of your projection, whether or not you deliver and if you do, what kind of impact you will ultimately have.

Two-Stroke Breath to Stimulate the Pituitary

Sit in easy pose with a straight spine. Put your thumbs on the mounds of Mercury. Keep the Jupiter (index) fingers extended and close the other 3 fingers over the thumb, holding it in place

☀ to Finish:

INHALE DEEPLY, hold the breath for 20 seconds as you squeeze your body inwardly from fiber to fiber. EXHALE like cannon fire. INHALE DEEPLY, hold the breath for 20 seconds as you put all the strength of the body into pressing the two Jupiter fingers together. "Press it to bring out a balance and central nerve strength." EXHALE. INHALE DEEPLY and hold the breath for 20 seconds as you pressurize all the muscles of the spinal column, one by one, from tailbone to the highest vertebra of the neck (this means the vertebra called C-1 where the neck connects to the skull). EXHALE and relax.

* With the right palm facing out and the left palm facing IN, touch the PADS of the 2 Jupiter fingers together, making a connection between them. THEY WILL FORM A "V" IN FRONT OF YOU.

* PLACE the mudra so that the tip of the "v" is about the level of the Root (bridge) of your nose. SLOWLY close your eyes so they are 9/10's closed and LOOK at the "V" with your "inner eye."

* INHALE Powerfully through the mouth in 2 strokes
  1 second per stroke = 2 second inhale

* EXHALE Powerfully through the nose in 2 strokes
  1 second per stroke = 2 second exhale.

* BReathe WITH your full strength for 11 min.

If you are looking for a standard of intuitive excellence... Yogi Bhajan said that you should be in a position to decide everything in one one-thousandth of a second.

DAILY ACTIONS

You must practice daily actions in order to make changes on the deepest spiritual and creative levels; the consistency resets the chain reactions that are deeply imbedded in the subconscious mind. In Kundalini Yoga, we call this daily practice sadhana; it is the cornerstone of all yoga and spiritual practices.

Creative Living and/or being an artist also involves daily actions that may or may not overlap with a spiritual sadhana. Showing up in the studio on a regular basis or "on the page" as some writers refer to it, are actions or rituals repeated over time with consistency. These are the techniques that bear the most fruit.

"One part of sadhana should stay constant long enough for you to master, or at least experience the changes evoked by a single technique. Each kriya and mantra has its individual effects, although they all elevate you toward a cosmic consciousness. Learn to value the pricelessness of one kriya, and all others will be understood in a clearer light."

If you are an artist or a creative person, you probably already perform some kind of discipline or ritual to get the juices flowing. Sweeping the floor and clearing the work space is something that many artists do (as well as shop owners in other parts of the world). Physical movement such as warm-ups, dancing, yoga, or a brisk walk before the workday begins is very helpful in getting the creative energy moving and releasing tension. Music can put you into a mental state conducive for creative work and for those who rely on it, creating playlists or playing certain pieces of music are extremely helpful. Some people need to write lists or mind-map to get the mental energy moving and organized. Having a "magical chair" or a "good-luck table" is not uncommon. I have my favorite tools, too …like my special palette knife and my favorite Exacto blade holder, both of which I've used for years. I know of writers who can only write with a certain kind of pencil on a particular brand of paper. These are just a few examples; I am sure you can come up with some of your own magic rituals.

These items and actions are talismans; they provide mental connection to the stream of creative intuition. **They work because we invented them and gave them power or we just believe in their power because of magical thinking.** Maybe that screenplay you just sold was written when you were sitting in that "magical chair"…you see what I'm getting at? Because all of these things are rooted outside of our selves, they are attachments, they are not real, and are therefore illusory. They are not bad, you don't have to "stop using them" in fact some of them are entirely practical, but it's good to recognize them for what they are. Ultimately, we don't want to create dependence on anything outside of our selves. We don't want to feel that we cannot create without our lucky charms.

What we do want to do is to create habits and daily actions that connect us to our strengths and gifts at will. This means that our inner strength, power, reverence and intuition are with us all the time so that we don't need to use something outside of our selves to facilitate connection. We can hook up with the creative flow when we want to because of our chakra alignment and the vibrational frequency of our aura.

We want to create a blueprint that is as real as we are. For many artists it just means showing up at the studio or being in the space of creation; just diving into the work and the process makes things occur. The artist Susan Rothenberg said that she shows up in her studio because she believes very strongly *"that if you're not in your studio physically most every day, you've denied the possibility of anything happening."*

and one of my favorite quotes on the subject from the painter Chuck Close:

"Inspiration is for amateurs. The rest of us just show up and get to work. If you wait around for the clouds to part and a bolt of lightening to strike you in the brain, you are not going to make an awful lot of work. All the best ideas come out of the process; they come out of the work itself."

All this brings me to the main point of this chapter which is how are you going to construct a plan for Creative Living that works for you and that you can do everyday? In a lot of ways, doing your daily actions is akin to showing up at the studio whether you have something "in the works" or not. You just show up and do it. Your daily spiritual practice is putting energy in the bank and investing in your future, and most important, making your NOW more creative, prosperous and productive.

Some people like to start new commitments full on and that method works fine for them. Jumping in the deep end is just one approach; I think there are factors that need to be considered if the gung-ho approach is your jam: How quickly do you need your progress to be? What is your age and how is your health? Do you have family or relational commitments? How can deepening your art or spiritual practice improve your life? How much time are you able or willing to devote to that end?

"What is the idea of commitment? Commitment makes you stronger and stronger. It gives you Shakti; you don't get Shakti from anything else. Shakti power, success, happiness, the source is one: commitment. And commitment is a power in itself."

What I find extremely helpful over the long haul, is beginning with what you can handle now. You can always increase and add on, but your chances of achieving a sustainable practice are greater if you start with what you can actually do on a consistent basis. Be honest with yourself. When you train for a marathon, you generally don't start with twenty-six miles.

Daily Do-Ability is the bottom line.

A daily yogic practice or sadhana is the highest form of self-care and maintaining a level of consistency is the key to successful self-care. Self-care is living in a conscious and responsible way so that you can flourish; making sure you get what you need to grow and function at your best all of the time. I am not talking about a "one-off" creative spiritual experience; I am talking about aligning yourself with Conscious Creativity for the long term. Commitment is everything; create a practice that points you in the direction you want to go and then start marching.

Here are four components of a recommended daily yogic practice. This teaching will take you far. If you hit these bullet points, you will have a respectable sadhana and it will show. Duration can vary according to time availability and physical ability. All four do not need to be done at once, and you can do multiples of each component if desired; for example, you can do more than one kriya or meditation or pranayama in the course of one day.

- Breathing consciously (pranayam) nurtures a relationship with Divine Consciousness. Connects you to the Creative Flow Channel.

- Chanting mantra is, according to Yogi Bhajan, "the mental vibratory projected thunderbolt of the human" and has the supreme power of making the mind and the neutral self one and the same. It's like a superfood for Creativity.

- Meditation will clear your subconscious mind so you can think better and will improve glandular and nervous system function so you can act better. Will help to relieve stress and improve creative function.

- Yogic exercise changes the blood chemistry and opens up the channels to receive and direct the creative flow. *Here's Yogi Bhajan on the subject: "Some people misunderstand about yogic exercises. Yogic exercises are not physical exercises at all, they do not mean anything physical, except they are tune-ups. Yoga exercises are meant for glandular system because glands are the guardians of the health."* The yoga kriyas open up blocks and move the Creative energy.

Here is some important information on timing. When we talk about meditation, many people have questions regarding the length of the meditations. "Why do we do this mediation for 11 minutes and this other meditation for 62 minutes? Yogi Bhajan was very specific in his instructions when necessary; for example he said for the Rejuvenation Meditation "under no circumstances should the meditation be practiced for more than 31 minutes" but in general he gave a range.

The general rule of thumb is that meditations and exercises can be practiced for any length of time less than the limit given - like if the instructions say "Chant for up to 5 minutes" or "sit quietly and meditate on the sound of the breath for 11 minutes", you could chant for 3 minutes or meditate for 8 minutes, respectively. But remember that a meditation or exercise should never be practiced for **more** than the time given.

Here's the Kundalini Yoga lowdown on the timing of meditations and the affect that it has:

✱*3 minutes of meditation affects the electromagnetic field, the circulation, and stability of the blood chemistry.*

✱11 minutes of meditation begins to change the nerves and the glandular system.

✱22 minutes of meditation balances the three minds (negative, positive, and neutral) and they start to work together so your mental integration changes.

✱31 minutes of meditation allows the glands, breath, and concentration to affect all the cells and rhythms of the body. It balances the 3 gunas, 31 tattvas, and all layers of the mind's projections.

✱62 minutes of meditation changes the gray matter in the brain. The subconscious mind and your positive projection are integrated.

＊2 ½ hours of meditation changes the psyche in relation to the surrounding magnetic field so that the subconscious mind is held firmly in the new pattern by the surrounding universal mind.

So are you now at the point where you are thinking, where do I begin? Figure out what you are trying to achieve or what you want to improve or work on? What are your basic four practices? Pranayam, mantra, yoga set and meditation.

What pranayam is do-able for you on a daily basis? Breath of Fire, Long Deep Breathing, One Minute Breath and the meditations that are based on breath patterns (included in this book) are all good choices.

What is your go-to mantra? In other words, what mantra comes to mind when you need assistance, protection, guidance? Chanting it throughout the day can really make a difference. Sat Nam and Wahe Guru are easy to remember and no less powerful because of their relative size. Repeating them (japa) on a mala is a great discipline. Look at the subchapter on Mantras for Creativity for ideas! Chant a mantra 108 times around your mala.

What physical yoga set is possible for you do every day? What is the sort of outcome you are looking for? How much time do you have? Most of the Kundalini Yoga kriyas can be practiced with less repetitions or time durations; the length of a yoga set could be anywhere from 15 to 45 minutes long depending on how long each individual exercise is practiced. Are there exercises in the kriya that you would benefit from without causing further injury to an existing condition? If I had a serious lower back issue, for example, I wouldn't be practicing a set that included 108 leg lifts…at least not right now….or I might practice that same set and do much fewer leg lifts! Believe me, there are plenty of navel-fortifying yoga sets to chose from that do not include leg lifts if that is an issue!

When thinking about choosing a meditation, you might ask yourself what sort of new habits do I want to install in my mind? What kind of progress do I want to make and how quickly? What meditation is do-able for me over the long term? If you want to feel the Infinite flow of the creative source in you, The Meditation for the Blossoming of the Self is a beautiful heart opening practice that brings a sense of Oneness. It's easy to do, doesn't require any long-held arm positions, and relies on your own natural breathing pattern as it aligns with the gentle movement of the hands. Other meditations might require repetitive physical movements, a concentrated eye focus, complicated breath patterns and those long-held durational arm positions I just mentioned a sentence ago.

There are a multitude of meditations to choose from; I included a bunch of the ones I am familiar with that I have used inside of the context of creativity. There are books that are filled with nothing but meditations and kriyas, and of course there are on-line resources like The Library of Teachings, 3HO, and RA MA TV. You might find kriyas or meditations in a class you attend…you just want to make sure that the teachings are authentic and originate from Kundalini Yoga as taught by Yogi Bhajan®.

The idea is to find a meditation that is **do-able, takes you where you want to go** and aim to **practice it for the recommended duration.** Most important is **to practice it consistently** - long enough for you to master it so that, as Yogi Bhajan said, *"you can experience the changes evoked by a single technique…Learn to value the pricelessness of one kriya, and all others will be understood in a clearer light."*

Your practice will include the Adi Mantra, Ong Namo Guru Dev Namo chanted three times to connect to the Golden Chain and to bow to the teacher within you.

A pranayam, a yoga kriya and your meditation will follow. Your mantra might be separate or included in either the kriya or the meditation. Relax…stretch…and either offer a prayer or chant the Long Time Sun and then Sat Nam which can be chanted one to three times.

May the Long Time Sun Shine Upon You, All Love Surround You, and the Pure Light Within You, Guide Your Way On….
SAT NAM

Here are 3 Creativity Hacks you could do if you just wanted to reboot your artistic self but weren't looking for a yogic practice, necessarily:

The Timer Trick - set a timer to a certain amount of minutes that you designate to creative play. The ultimate goal is to give yourself ninety minutes a day, but I suggest you start with fifteen and work up unless you are the type that likes to jump in the deep end. In these precious minutes, you are not allowed to use social media or talk on the phone and you must focus on just being "creative" whatever that means to you. Dance, write, paint, doodle, sing…whatever you do, and it doesn't have to be the same every day, do it in the spirit of play. No judgement. No comparison. You are just using the time for YOU to explore your creativity. It's not as easy as it sounds at first, but it turns into a real joy once you experience the time as yours and yours alone.

Crop Rotation: (Joni Mitchell's teaching) Many people think that they have to make art in one way; that if you identify as a painter, you must always paint. Just like a farmer plants different crops in the same land, it is advised that you do the same with your art-making. The more you switch things up, the better flow you're going to get. If you dry up as a poet, rather than feeling angst about it, you might find creative fertility as a sculptor or a dancer. Be open to trying new things. All roads lead to Rome…

Enjoy the creative processes of others: Visit museums, galleries and make studio visits. Go to the theatre, the symphony, the ballet. Experience live music anywhere, go to alternative performance spaces, visit public gardens, site-specific art installations and architectural space. Take lessons in something you are curious about from someone you admire.

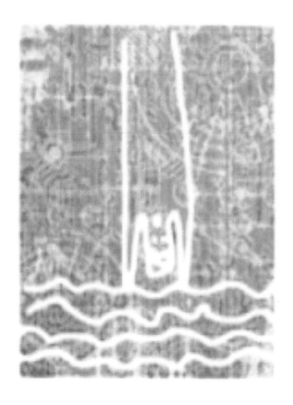

RISK TAKING

There is much to be learned and attained from becoming our own own laboratory. Yogi Bhajan had this to say on the subject:

"Those who take the risk, gain. Those who do not take the risk, have already lost. It isn't the life that matters. It is the courage you bring to it."

There isn't a successful creative person out there who hasn't had to take risks. The whole business of making things out of nothing is 100% unadulterated going out on a ledge ... jumping out of a airplane without a parachute ...walking the tight rope without a safety net. Creatives fail all the time and those who do really well for themselves, fail even more than that! The most creative people have the most output...that doesn't mean that every creative idea is a home run, they just have more creative output to choose from.

Creativity not only requires courage and a belief in ones ideas, it also requires a willingness to go out on that ledge for them time and time again. **Neurologically speaking, creativity is the by-product of our brains making long distance connections.**

Let's say we have a problem and we go about solving it in our usual fashion… So here we are, thinking about our problem and we are busy looking for the solution in, metaphorically speaking, the Google search engine in our brain. We all know that Google has its limitations and operates on algorithms which narrow the search; thereby keeping you from getting overloaded with too much information and too many options. The results of your search are targeted to your demographic and previous search history so the solution to your problem is pretty much a predictable one.

On the other hand, when creative people solve the same problem, they don't just search with Google and the familiar databases; they go on a treasure hunt looking for unusual connections in the hidden places of their brain, creating unexpected relationships between unrelated things, and poking around in the subtle hiding places where the mysteries of the universe reside. In other words, their search engine doesn't operate within the narrow algorithm of limited and predictable information. In fact, their brains go where they may never have gone before…This is why most creative people are fearless in ways "normal" people are not.

One way you can engender creativity in a person who doesn't believe they are creative is to get them to take risks. Risk taking is a muscle that has to be exercised. Risk taking causes the brain to stretch it muscles so it can think in unusual unexpected ways. Risk taking warms you up so you can participate in Creative Living.

While trying out a new choreography may not be physically as dangerous or thrilling as bungee jumping, it still activates the risk hormone, adrenaline. Before any project, you might feel that tinge of the fear of the unknown and that urge and willingness to go the distance. If you don't have that adrenaline "charge", your heart and soul is probably not invested.

During the flourishing stage of a project, the risk shows up in the adrenaline rush of new discoveries and the unexpected surprises that surface in the process of creation. We start to get excited and nervous about bringing the project forth, and this forces us to go deeper into the work and expand beyond our fears.

When the project is ready to be brought forth and in the case of our choreography example, performed in front of an audience, that is where the feeling of risk escalates and can be, for some a crippling experience. It is most crucial at this point in any creative venture to follow through on your intention and deliver it.

I mentioned this before, but that nervous adrenaline feeling which we interpret as performance anxiety, is just the powerful energy of the investment that your heart and soul have made.

The risk muscles must be used and the more you use them, the stronger they get and the more creative you become. If you are already a successful creative person, you can always improve on your risk taking skills.

One of the greatest outcomes of a dedicated Kundalini Yoga practice is the elimination of fear and worry and the increase in courageousness and self-confidence. If you needed to work on fearlessness and taking more risks, I would suggest starting with conscious breathing.

Becoming aware of your breath can change your world

"You start conscious breathing and you have all the answers. You breathe consciously: you inhale consciously, you exhale consciously, and you'll get all the answers. So long you are unconsciously breathing, you are unconsciously living. What is the idea of conscious breathing? With conscious breathing you can work and you can talk, but you are always into that Self of that Creator as a creature. You enjoy the unison-ness of God within you. You and the Supreme Self are united. That is the character we all have to build to survive."

Yogi Bhajan

Creativity thrives on taking risks... in fact without risk, there is no creativity.

AND ONE LAST THING...

In 2013 I began a project called 120 Days of Amplitude. It was my goal to set up a creative laboratory and use myself as the guinea pig. It was the start of my thinking that a daily practice taken on for the specific purpose of connecting to the creative flow could enhance my creative output and that practicing specific kriyas and meditations that sparked the creative fire, could make a big difference. You could say it was the seed for The Blueprint for Creativity.

I wanted to see just how creatively productive and focused I could be if I combined my spiritual practice and my artistic practice into an eight hour work day (minimum) over the period of four months of consistent daily practice.

The outcome was pretty phenomenal in many ways.

First, I was able to raise funds through a Creative Arts crowdfunding platform called USA PROJECTS (a program created by United States Artists (USA), which is a nonprofit grant making and artist advocacy organization) to subsidize my four months of concentrated creative and yogic work which helped to pay for materials, studio space, and so on.

Second, I had many insights about the nature of creative work and spiritual work. To chronicle my progress, I wrote a blog and posted entries on social media. Here is an entry from around two months in:

"The meditation is helping the painting a lot and the painting is helping the meditation. Meditation is creative and Painting is a meditation. Both are skills. Both are arts. Both require concentration and self-discipline. Both are scary. Both are tremendously rewarding. But together they've pushed me into a whole new realm of awareness."

Every morning (in addition to my regular sadhana four hours earlier) I started my workday with the Meditation for Healing Addictions, a nine minute meditation called The Base of Your Creative Capacity for Life from the Self-Knowledge book. I then did a short yoga set (which I changed every few days or so) followed by 31 minutes of the Laya Yoga Kundalini Mantra. The whole 120 Days of Amplitude yoga practice took about an hour to an hour and a half.

I swear by The Base of Your Creative Capacity for Life and The Laya Yoga Kundalini Mantra as two practices that will give you RADICAL CREATIVITY in a relatively short amount of time. One of the benefits of the Laya Yoga is that is makes you creative and focused on your real priorities and helps you to sacrifice what is needed to accomplish them. The Addiction Meditation holds everything in balance.

How many times have you set out to achieve a creative goal and have been sidetracked by some activity you "suddenly" had to do or an invitation to do something during your designated creative time? That distract-ability and procrastination can stop if you want it to just by practicing Laya Yoga Kundalini Mantra. Just sayin'.

THE BASE OF YOUR CREATIVE CAPACITY FOR LIFE

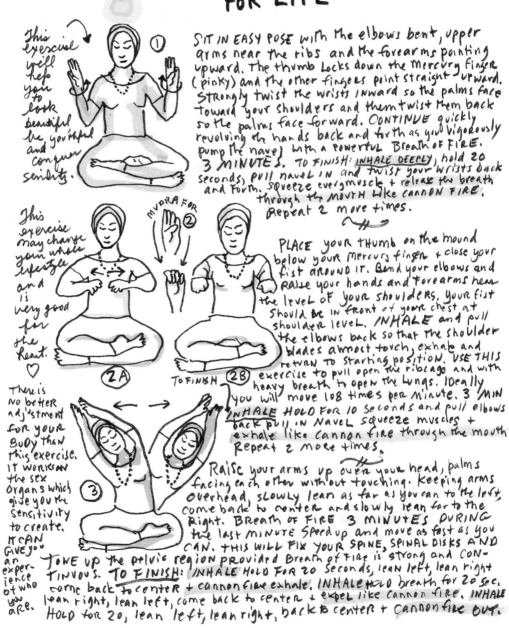

This exercise will help you to look beautiful, be youthful and conquer senility.

SIT IN EASY POSE with the elbows bent, upper arms near the ribs and the forearms pointing upward. The thumb locks down the Mercury finger (pinky) and the other fingers point straight upward. Strongly twist the wrists INWARD so the palms face toward your shoulders and them twist them back so the palms face forward. CONTINUE quickly revolving the hands back and forth as you vigorously pump the navel with a powerful Breath of FIRE. 3 MINUTES. TO FINISH: _INHALE DEEPLY_, hold 20 seconds, pull navel IN and twist your wrists back and forth. Squeeze every muscle + release the breath through the mouth like CANNON FIRE. Repeat 2 more times.

This exercise may change your whole lifestyle and is very good for the heart. ♥

MUDRA FOR ②

PLACE your thumb on the mound below your Mercury finger + close your fist around it. Bend your elbows and raise your hands and forearms near the level of your shoulders. Your fist should be in front of your chest at shoulder level. INHALE and pull the elbows back so that the shoulder blades almost touch, exhale and return to starting position. USE THIS exercise to pull open the ribcage and with heavy breath to open the lungs. Ideally you will move 108 times per minute. 3 MIN INHALE HOLD FOR 10 seconds and pull elbows back pull in Navel squeeze muscles + exhale like cannon fire through the mouth Repeat 2 more times.

②A   TO FINISH ②B

There is no better adjustment for your body than this exercise. It works on the sex organs which give you the sensitivity to create. IT CAN GIVE you an experience of who you are.

Raise your arms up over your head, palms facing each other without touching. Keeping arms overhead, slowly lean as far as you can to the left, come back to center and slowly lean far to the right. BREATH of FIRE 3 MINUTES DURING the last MINUTE speed up and move as fast as you CAN. THIS WILL FIX YOUR SPINE, SPINAL DISKS AND TONE up the pelvic region provided Breath of fire is strong and CONTINUOUS. TO FINISH: INHALE HOLD FOR 20 seconds, lean left, lean right come back to center + cannon fire exhale. INHALE HOLD breath for 20 sec. lean right, lean left, come back to center + expel like cannon fire. INHALE HOLD for 20, lean left, lean right, back to center + cannon fire OUT.

③

LAYA YOGA KUNDALINI MANTRA

SIT IN EASY POSE WITH A Light jalandhar bandh (neck lock)

EYE POSITION: Focus through the brow Point

MUDRA: Put palms together at center of the chest OR IN GYAN MUDRA with the wrists on the knees.

MANTRA & VISUALIZATION:

• one creator creation. EK ONG KAAR- (UH)

• True Identity•   SAA TAA NAA MAA

• great indescribable wisdom• SIREE WHAA - (UH) HAY GU-ROO

The chant is very precise. ON EK pull IN the navel. ON each final "UH" lift the diaphragm up firmly. The "UH" sound is more a result of the powerful movement of the diaphragm than a pronounced purposeful projected SOUND. Relax the navel and abdomen on HAY GUROO. The sound has a "spin" to it. It's a 3-½ Cycle RHYTHM. As you chant, imagine energy and sound SPIRALING UP and around the SPINAL CORD IN A Right handed helix. Start at the base of the spine as you initiate the energy from the NAVEL. END WITH THE FOCUS over the head to the COSMOS on HAY-GUROO.

TIME: CONTINUE FOR 31 MINUTES. Practice for 40-120 days.

Comments: This extraordinary Laya Yoga chant brings the soul and destiny present. It suspends you above conflicts attracted by success and the activity of the Positive Mind. It lets your activity serve your purpose. It makes you creative and focused on your real priorities and helps you sacrifice what is needed to accomplish them.

COMMENTS **CONTINUED**: The word Laya refers to suspension from the ordinary world. Laya Yoga fixes your attention and energy on your essence and higher consciousness without normal distractions and attachments having power over your reactive awareness.

This mantra opens the secret book of Laya Yoga. It enables you to consciously remember and experience the link between you and the Creator. Practice the mantra for 40-120 days. It will etch in your sub-conscious the memory and experience of your true identity.

This mantra was guarded like a secret gem. It is the key to the inner doors of NAAD, the realm of creative sound. If you listen to the sound of the mantra, and then concentrate into its subtle sounds, you will become absorbed into the Unlimited Domain of your higher self. The mantra has a structure of 3-1/2 cycles in its spin. Each UH sound lifts the diaphragm which commutes the energy of prana an apana across the heart area. That transformation is one cycle. The 3-1/2 cycle is the PULSE RHYTHM of the kundalini itself. This is why the kundalini is often represented as coiled 3-1/2 times.

As with all other genuine mantras, it is discovered by the seer who travels in the subtle realms of consciousness. It has been confirmed by countless practitioners who adapted the discipline of meditation. The inner sounds can be heard at different levels of subtlety. The vibrations of NAAD have different octaves of creative IMPACT. This mantra takes you to the MOST SUBTLE REALM of creativity. It awakens the kundalini force that energizes the whole CREATION. It awakens YOUR awareness and empowers the sense of the subtle Body & the AURA. IT also gives INTUITION and the Power to HEAL.

When you practice this KRIYA earestly, be conscious and graceful with each WORD you speak. DO NOT listen to negative or coarse speech from others. Remember that the SINS of the past are of the past and that some of the greatest saints were sinners first. If you have the opportunity to learn and to practice this technology of elevation, you have earned it and you deserve it. So do not hesitate to use it and to sTRive for progress and EXPANSION. FEEL that the Infinite Will and yours act together. Strong action combined with non-attachment make life a dance with much CREATIVITY and gratitude.

Sat Nam

© YOGI BHAJAN

MEDITATION FOR HEALING ADDICTIONS

PRACTICE IT AND SEE WHAT HAPPENS!

SIT IN EASY POSE WITH A LIGHT JALANDHAR BANDH (NECK LOCK) STRAIGHTEN THE SPINE AND make sure the FIRST SIX Lower vertebrae are locked FORWARD.

EYE POSITION: Keep the eyes Closed AND focused at the brow point.

MANTRA: SAA-TAA-NAA-MAA

MUDRA: make fists of both hands and extend the thumbs straight. Place the thumbs on the temples and find the "niche" where the thumbs just fit. this is the Lower anterior portion of the frontal bone above the temporal-sphenoidal sutre. LOCK THE BACK MOLARS together and keep the LIPS CLOSED. Keeping the teeth pressed together throughout, alternately squeeze the MOLARS tightly and then release the pressure. A muscle will move in Rhythm under the thumbs. Feel it massage the thumbs and apply a firm pressure with the hands. Silently VIBRATE the 5 PRIMAL SOUNDS— the PANJ SHABD SAA-TAA-NAA-MAA at the BROW.

TIME: CONTINUE for 5-7 minutes. With practice, the time can be increased to 20 minute and ULTimately to 31 minutes.

Comments: the pressure exerted by the thumbs triggers a Rhythmic Refley current Into the Central Brain. this current activates the bRain area directy underneath the stem of the pineal gland. It is an imbalance in this area that makes mental and physical addictions seemingly unbreakable. THIS meditation CORRects THis imbalance.

NOTES AND ADDITIONAL PRACTICES

There is so much information that I have collected over the years from various sources and since this is not an academic paper, I am not going to cite each and every quote or entry. Of course, the majority of the material in this book came from Yogi Bhajan's lectures that are archived on The Library of Teachings as I mentioned on my gratitude page up front.

I also referred to the 3HO website often and relied heavily on my own lecture notes and all my yoga and "art" books; some of which include, but are not limited to the Aquarian Teacher Level One course books; old issues of The Beads of Truth and Aquarian Times, the spiral bound manuals that were complied and illustrated by Harijot Kaur Khalsa like Physical Wisdom, Reaching Me in Me, Self-Knowledge, and so on; the lectures from The Master's Touch that were all transcribed and compiled by the incomparable Tej Kaur Khalsa; Kundalini Yoga: The Flow of Eternal Power by Shakti Parwha Kaur Khalsa (a true classic); the must-have Praana, Praanee, Praanayam compiled and illustrated by Harijot Kaur Khalsa; The Mind: Its projections and Multiple Facets by Yogi Bhajan; Fountain of Youth - teachings compiled by Sumpuran Khalsa and illustrated by Wahe Guru Kaur; The Ancient Art of Self-Healing by Yogi Bhajan; Yoga for Youth and Joy by Yogi Bhajan; The Conscious Activist by James O'Dea; True Perception: The Path of Dharma Art by Chögyam Trungpa; Subtle Activism by David Nicol, The Buddha Mind in Contemporary Art edited by Jacquelyn Bass and Mary Jane Jacob; The BrainyQuote

and GoodReads websites for the things people say;
YouTube videos of artists talking that I
transcribed; the Womens Camp Teaching Manuals....
Education for Socially Engaged Art: materials and
techniques handbook by Pablo Helguera; Essays on the
Blurring of Art and Life by Allan Kaprow; Deep
Listening: A Composers Sound Practice by Pauline
Oliveros; and Writing as Sculpture: 1978-1987 by
Louwrien Wijers...plus tons of articles from research
papers and on-line blogs. Each and every one of the
books on the list has spent a lot of time on my
kitchen and bedside tables.

Here are four more articles, publications and videos I referenced:

Tippett, Krista. "Meredith Monk - Archaeologist of the Human Voice -." On Being with Krista Tippett.

Rosenberg, Jeremy. "Hirokazu Kosaka: From a Buddhist Monastery in Japan to an Art Legend in L.A." KCET. March 15, 2012

Oliveros, Pauline. Deep Listening: A Composer's Sound Practice. NY: IUniverse, Inc., 2005.

Knowles, Alison, Eleanor Heartney, Meredith Monk, Linda Montano, Erik Ehn, and Bonnie Marranca. "Art as Spiritual Practice." PAJ: A Journal of Performance and Art 24, no. 3 (September 2002)

If any of the artists or spiritual teachers and masters I wrote about in the Eleven Yogic Arts of Creative Living spark your interest or if any the quotes makes you want to learn more about the person, I suggest you dig deeper. Many of the people I write about hold spirituality and creativity in perfect balance and there is much to learn from them.

I hope this book ignites your self-discipline and your passion to know more about this subject.

Regarding Yogi Bhajan's quotes:

In case you were wondering, whenever there is an isolated quote by Yogi Bhajan, I have decided to always use the font, Ana's Rusty Typewriter (which I am using now). It reminds me of the old write-ups and the Women's Camp Notes and also I am from the time way back when, when I used to actually have a typewriter like this one. It had the ability to type in both black and red by using a split ribbon. I'm getting into this little bit of nostalgia here...

Tuning in:

When beginning a Kundalini Yoga Practice, it's important to tune in.

Ong Namo Guru Dev Namo: Adi Mantra

This mantra is to be chanted at least three times before every class or practice session of Kundalini Yoga, meditation or chanting. The Adi Mantra opens the protective channel of energy for Kundalini Yoga; the Golden Chain. Ong is the infinite creative energy manifested in earthly form and activity. Namo means "I bow." Guru is the teacher who transmits the technology of wisdom. Dev is the Etheric Divinity of God. The meaning of the mantra is: "I bow to the Infinite Creative Consciousness. I bow to the Divine Wisdom within and without."

This mantra is chanted in Easy Pose with the hands in Prayer Mudra, - thumbs pressing in slightly above the sternum. The eyes are closed and focused at the third eye point. The word Ong is vibrated powerfully through the nose , and there is a quick half breath taken between the first Namo and Guru. You can also chant it with one breath.

Ong . . . .   Namo . . . .   Gu-roo Dev . . .   Na-mo . . . .

Basic Sitting Postures:

Easy Pose:

Sit up with both legs straight. Put one foot under the opposite knee and then draw the extended foot under the other knee. Pull the spine up straight and press the lower spine slightly forward.

Rock Pose (Vajrasana):

This asana is well known for its beneficial effects on the digestive system. It gained its nickname from the idea that one who masters this posture can sit in it and "digest rocks." It also makes you solid and balanced as a rock.

To get in the position start by kneeling on both knees with the top of the feet on the ground. Sit back on the heels. The heels will press the two nerves that run into the lower center of each buttock. Keep the spine pulled straight.

Chair Yoga:

Kundalini Yoga can also be practiced sitting in a chair. If you practice a meditation in a chair, be sure to keep your feet flat on the ground. Yoga kriyas can be modified for those who cannot sit on the floor.

Concluding an exercise:

Unless otherwise stated, an exercise is concluded by inhaling and holding the breath briefly, then exhaling and relaxing the posture. While the breath is being held, apply the mulbandha or root lock, contracting the muscles around the sphincter, the sex organs, and the navel point. This consolidates the effects of any exercise and circulates the energy to your higher centers. Do not hold the breath to the point of dizziness. If you start to feel dizzy or faint, immediately exhale and relax.

The Relaxation between exercises:

An important part of any exercise is the relaxation following it. Unless otherwise specified, you should allow one to three minutes of relaxation in easy pose or lying on the back in corpse pose after each exercise. The less experienced you are or the more strenuous the exercise, the longer the relaxation period should be. Some sets end with a period of "deep relaxation" which may extend from three to ten minutes.

Cat Cow:

This is a 2-part exercise done on all fours. Exhale as the spine is arched up and the head down (cat pose). (A) Inhale as the spine is arched and relaxed down and the head up (cow pose). (B) ,

This is considered a complete kriya and has a multitude of benefits some of which include: keeping the spine young and flexible, clears emotional debris and blockages, increases circulation, increases lung capacity, builds the pranic reserves, calms and focuses the mind, and lots more.

Breath of Fire and cat/cow - together - are a great warm-up before your practice and they are an excellent pre-amble to a meditation if you don't have time for a full-on yoga set. (the breath of fire would be considered a pranayam and the cat/cow, a complete kriya.

On the subject of "warm-ups", besides cat/cow, spinal flexes and life nerve stretches are good, too.

How do you conclude a Kundalini Yoga set?

After doing a series of exercises and/or your meditation, you give yourself a relaxation period. You will find that if you do the following exercises after you relax, it will bring you back to reality and help to ground you:

1) On your back. begin rotating your feet and hands in small circles. Continue in one direction for about 30 seconds, then in the other direction for another 30 seconds or so.

2) Still on your back rub the soles of the feet and the palms of the hands together briskly. creating a sensation of heat. Continue for up to 1 minute.

3) Cat stretch: Keeping both shoulders and the left leg flat on the ground. bring the right arm back behind the head and the right knee over the left leg till it touches the floor on the far side of the body.(27) Switch legs and arms and repeat the exercise.

4) Clasping knees to chest with both hands. begin rolling on the spine side to side. Then roll all the way back till the feet touch the ground behind the head one all the way forward until you are sitting up...that is, if you can otherwise just rock up and down like a rocking horse... Do this 3

or 4 times each. This is a great massage for your vertebrae.

5) Sit up in easy pose. Palms together in prayer mudra at the heart center. Eyes are closed. Inhale completely and say a prayer of thanks or chant Long Time Sun one to three times. Let it all go... and chant long Sat Nam 3x.

All the illustrations in this book were done by me... except for this one.

This is a portrait of me with my daughter Zoë inside.

According to this book, in this drawing, I am in the Flourishing Stage of Creativity.

Zoë drew that of us when she was very young... like about three years old.

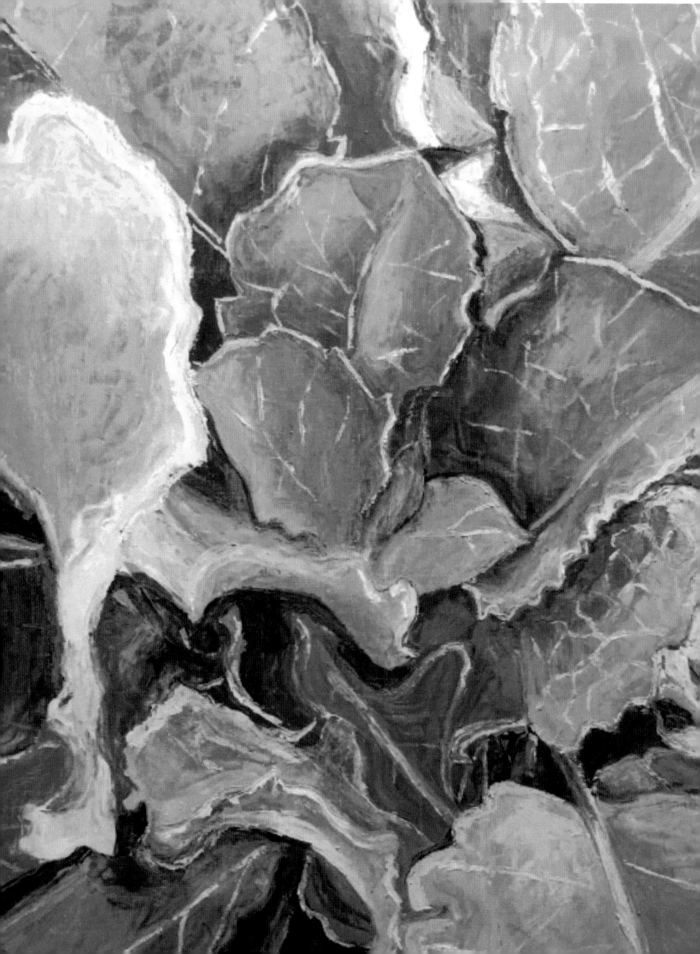

ARTWORK BY RAGHUBIR KHALSA KINTISCH

page 68
Heavenly Father, 1994, oil on canvas, 38 x 50" (detail of self-portrait)

page 79
GS's Hand Of Infinity, 2019, ink and media on paper, 10 x 15"

page 267
The Sustainer, 2019, oil on linen, 50 x 62"

page 279
Big Saltbush, 2017, oil on linen, 50 x 62"

page 284
Echo Park Camphor Tree, 2013, oil on canvas, 24 x 30" (part of 120 Days of Amplitude project)

page 287
The Three Graces, ink on paper, 2019, 10 x 15"

page 288
Intravision Project/11 Yogic Arts Mindmap, 2016-2020, digital

ALL ILLUSTRATIONS BY RKK

PHOTOGRAPHY

Cover Photograph by Marla Strick at the Noguchi
Museum, Long Island City, New York, 2017

page 2
RKK by Carla Coffing at the Moon Sanctuary in
Atwater Village, Los Angeles, 2020

page 3
Pomegranate Vendor in India by RKK, 2013

pg 7
3HO Website

pg 10
Early Artist in the Bronx, circa 1957 by Irving
Kintisch

pg 8, 12, 13
Teaching at Summer Solstice, me and big photo of SSS,
and playing accordion at Follow Your Heart by Elena
Tchoujtchenko

pg 14
RKK at the Golden Temple by Santosh Kaur Khalsa,
2008

pg 31
RKK at Fort Ticonderoga by Irving Kintisch, 1960

"The problem with walking on the spiritual path is that you are tested at every step. Each step expands you, lifts you, and gives you elevation. But on the neurotic path, the path of ego, you enjoy every step, but every step is just flat. No lift, no elevation. You get so tied into it that soon nothing can reach you. Ego is the very capacity to be finite. You say, "I am. These are my things. This is my life. Nobody can tell me anything. I'll do whatever I want to do." In the end it confines you tremendously and tragically. You give no attention to your destiny and lose perspective. You live life through the mind's reactions; you do not feel you as you. You do not penetrate to the soul and live from your heart. You avoid the tests and never gain your uniqueness in your destiny. The immediate pleasures of the ego cut you out of the picture and drag you away from the soul. Choose that path and you will never penetrate through your own mind and see the light of the soul, which is the part of God that is in you."

Yogi Bhajan

"YOUR SELF IS THE ONLY CONSCIOUS VOICE YOU HAVE, DEEP WITHIN YOU. DEVELOP THE HABIT TO LISTEN TO YOURSELF WHENEVER YOU ARE CONFRONTED WITH ANYTHING. TELL YOURSELF, THROUGH A MEDITATIVE MIND, "I MUST LISTEN TO MYSELF." IT IS THE FIRST STEP OF FRIENDSHIP BETWEEN THE BODY AND THE SOUL."

YOGI BHAJAN

INTRAVISION PROJECT

A LIVING SYLLABUS IN INTRAVISIONARY CREATIVE BEING

ART & CREATIVE PRACTICE ⟷ SPIRITUAL PRACTICE

Universal Mind

UPLINK — CONNECT

OBSERVATION AND LISTENING
FOCUS - WHAT ARE MY RESOURCES?
SELF-DISCIPLINE

ORIGIN OF IDEAS
INSPIRATION ?
MODES OF RESEARCH
COLLABORATION
EGO-LESSNESS

COSMIC DOWNLOADING
MEDITATION PRACTICES
MODES OF RESEARCH
UNIVERSAL MIND
EGO-LESSNESS

LISTENING
STILLING AND CONTROLLING THE MIND
SELF DISCIPLINE

CONCEIVE — GENERATE

PANEL DISCUSSIONS
COLLABORATIVE CREATIVITY
CONSCIOUSNESS RAISING
CROWDSOURCED SHARING
ONE ON ONE LIVE VIDEO INTERVIEWS
RECORDED INFO

ORGANIZATION OF MATERIAL
AND PREPARATION
IMPLANTING AN IDEA SEED
TRANSLATION OF IDEAS INTO POSSIBLE ACTIONS
CONVERSATIONS, WORKSHOPS
NUCLEUS OF CREATIVE PROJECT

ORGANIZATION AND READYING THE MIND
TO RECEIVE THOUGHT WAVES
TRANSLATION OF THOUGHT WAVES INTO IDEAS
TRANSLATION OF IDEAS INTO POSSIBLE ACTIONS
CONVERSATIONS, WORKSHOPS
NUCLEUS OF CREATIVITY

SPIRITUAL PRACTICE
YOGA AND MEDITATION
INVOLVING APPLICATOIN OF
TIME-BASED ACTIONS
OR SCORES
(IE, SPECIFIC YOGA SETS
AND MEDITATION)
WORKSHOPS

FLOURISH — ORGANIZE / PRODUCE

APPLICATION OF
TIME-BASED SCORES
ASSEMBLY OF RESEARCH INTO "ART"
TRANSCRIPTION OR TRANSLATION

BLOSSOMING OF IDEA SEED
ANALYZING AND UTILIZING RESEARCH
NURTURING AND DEVELOPMENT OF MATERIAL
DEVELOPING AND UTILIZING TIMELINES
HOW TO DISTRIBUTE, SHARE, EXHIBIT, PERFORM?
SEEKING FUNDING AND SUPORT

BUD TO BLOSSOM METABOLIC CHANGE OCCURS
INSATIABLE APPETITE FOR SELF-DISCOVERY
TRANSFORM "LOWER" ENERGY INTO "HIGHER" ENERGY
UTILIZE TIMELINES TO CHANGE HABITS - CREATE INFLOW
ANALYZE SELF PROGRESS THROUGH INCREASED AWARENESS
LIVE FROM THE HEART - INCREASED DESIRE TO SHARE
ACTION PLAN- DAILY PRACTICE -COMMUNITY SUPPORT

IMPROVED HEALTH
INCREASED ENERGY
LESS STRESS
LESS FEAR
UNISONNESS
CONTENTMENT
INCREASED CREATIVITY
BETTER COMMUNICATION

DELIVER — DESTROY OR DISRUPT

PERFORMATIVE ACTIONS
SOCIAL MEDIA
EVENTS
CONVERSATIONS
PODCAST
WORKSHOPS

RESULT OF ENERGETIC DETERMINATION
HOW DOES THE WORK REPRESENT YOU?
DESTRUCTION VERSUS DELIVERY
WHAT IS THE METHOD OF DELIVERY? WHO IS YOUR AUDIENCE?
HOW VISABLE, VOCAL, ACCESSIBLE, ACTIVE ARE YOU/YOUR PROJECT?

RESULT OF ENERGETIC DETERMINATION
YOU ARE WHAT YOU DELIVER
DESTRUCTION VERSUS DELIVERY
HOW DO YOU DELIVER?
HOW VISABLE, VOCAL, ACCESSIBLE, ACTIVE ARE YOU?

CLASSES AND WORKSHOPS
SOCIAL MEDIA
EVENTS
VIDEOS
PUBLIC ACCESS

IMPACT — EFFECTIVE REPURCUSSIONS

ACTIVISM
PUBLIC PARTICIPATION
FEEDBACK
COMPASSION AND EMPATHY EXERCISES

IS A PROJECT ETHICAL, GOOD FOR OTHERS?
WHAT IS THE DESIRED OUTCOME?
QUANTITY OR QUALITY?
IS IT ABOUT SOMETHING OR DOES IT *DO* SOMETHING?
IS IT SUSTAINABLE? CAN IT BE REPRODUCED?
CAN YOU HANDLE THE EFFECT OF YOUR IMPACT?

CREATING IMPACT IS CREATIVITY'S PURPOSE
WHAT IS THE DESIRED OUTCOME?
WHO WILL BE AFFECTED AND HOW?
QUANTITY OR QUALITY?
CAN YOU HANDLE THE EFFECT OF YOUR IMPACT?
KARMIC IMPACT - EVERY ACTION HAS A REACTION
LIFE IS HELD BY IMPACT AND FED BY INFLOW

ACTIVISM
PUBLIC PARTICIPATION
FEED BACK AND SHARING

HEALING — PROCESS-BASED CONTINUOUS ACTION

OBSERVATION
LISTENING
STORYTELLING
EMPATHY

OBSERVATION
LISTENING
STORYTELLING
EMPATHY

COMPASSION
OPENING UP OF THE HEART
SENSE OF INFINITE CONNECTION
ACTIVATION OF HEALING ENERGY

SELF-CARE — PERSONAL SUSTAINABILITY

OUTCOME OF PRACTICAL PROJECTS
SELF ASSESSMENT
PROJECT ASSESSMENT
EXPERIENTIAL LEARNING
HOW TO KEEP GOING

SELF-NOURISHING PROJECTS
SELF-NOURISHING RITUALS
TIME AND ENERGY MANAGEMENT
TIMELINES AND REALISTIC GOAL SETTING
SELF REFLECTION
COMPASSION
FILLING THE WELL

SELF-NOURISHING RITUALS
PROMOTING HABITS NOT DEMOTING HABITS
DISCIPLINE -ONGOING PRACTICE
REASONABLE GOALS AND OUTCOMES
SELF-REFLECTION
COMPASSION
FILLING THE WELL

GAGING OUTCOME OF PRACTICE
SELF ASSESSMENT
LEARN THROUGH EXPERIENCE
DISCIPLINE - WHAT DO I NEED TO KEEP UP
PRACTICE OF PROMOTING HABITS
REMOVAL OF DEMOTING HABITS

PROSPERITY — SHARING

TEACHING AS ART
LIVING AS ART
SHARING AS ART

WHAT DO YOU HAVE THAT YOU CAN SHARE -
LOCATION, TALENT, MONEY, TIME, IDEAS
SELFLESS SERVICE
TEACHING - MENTORING

WHAT DO YOU HAVE THAT YOU CAN SHARE -
LOCATION, TALENT, MONEY, TIME, IDEAS
SELFLESS SERVICE - SEVA
TEACHING MENTORING

TEACHING AS ART
LIVING AS ART
SHARING AS ART
GETTING ENERGY BY GIVING

COMMUNITY — GROUP CONSCIOUNESS

WHAT DO WE HAVE IN COMMON?
WHERE DO WE DIFFER?
HOW CAN WE IDENTIFY ORDER IN CHAOS
UNIVERSAL MIND

THE ROLE OF OTHERS
PARTICIPANTS, AUDIENCE, VIEWERS,
CO-CREATORS, INTERPRETERS,
WITNESSES, ACTORS
GROUP DOCUMENTATION
GROUP REFLECTION
BUILDING GROUP DYNAMIC
STRENGTH IN NUMBERS

THE ROLE OF OTHERS
ROLE OF THE SANGAT
COMPANY,~FELLOWSHIP~ASSOCIATION
GROUP DOCUMENTATION
GROUP REFLECTION
HOLDING SPACE FOR GROUP DYNAMIC
SUBTLE ACTIVISM

COMMONALITY
POWER OF GROUP ENERGY FIELD
ACKNOWLEDGE DIFFERENCES
SUBTLE ACTIVISM STARTS WITH YOU
ORGANIZING
TEACHING - HOLDING CONSCIOUS EVENTS
ENCOURAGING DIVERSITY

Universal Mind

ten energetic bodies

CREATIVE INTELLIGENCE -
HOW CAN THE PROJECT
BE OF BENEFIT TO ALL
INVOLVED

BIRTH OF CREATIVITY — SOUL
PROTECTION-DISCERNMENT — NEGATIVE MIND
PROJECTION-IMAGINING — POSITIVE MIND
COMPASSIONATE INTELLIGENCE — NEUTRAL MIND
MANIFESTATION AND PRODUCTION — PHYSICAL BODY
SELF-CONFIDENCE AND POSITIVE PROJECTION — ARCLINE
AURA
ENERGY ACCESS AND MAINTENANCE — PRANIC BODY
POWERFUL SENSITIVITY — SUBTLE BODY
SUSTAINABILITY — RADIANT BODY

BIRTH OF CREATIVITY
PROTECTION-DISCERNMENT
PROJECTION-IMAGINING
COMPASSIONATE INTELLIGENCE
MANIFESTATION AND PRODUCTION
SELF-CONFIDENCE AND POSITIVE PROJECTION

ENERGY ACCESS AND MAINTENANCE
POWERFUL SENSITIVITY
SUSTAINABILITY

BRING ART TO SPIRITUAL
INSTITUTIONS AND SPIRITUALITY
TO ART INSITUTIONS

CREATIVE INTELLIGENCE -
HOW CAN THE PROJECT
BE OF BENEFIT TO ALL
INVOLVED

Striped Dog Press
Los Angeles, CA

The **Eleven Yogic Arts of Creative Living** is based on Kundalini Yoga as taught by Yogi Bhajan® and all the exercises and meditations were given to us by him somewhere between the early 1970's until 2004 when he left his body. They are not a substitute for medical care and the use of the technology and instructions in this book is taken at your own risk.

Just remember that the exercises and meditations interspersed throughout this book are designed to be safe for most people, provided that the directions are followed carefully. There are many benefits from doing these centuries-old yogic practices and the results will vary from person to person based on physical differences and the consistency and and accuracy of practice.

The publisher, author, and editor disclaim all liability in connection with the use of this information in individual cases. If you have any concerns about a particular exercise or meditation please consult a certified KRI Kundalini Yoga teacher who has experience and is equipped to guide you. If you have any medical concerns, please go see your doctor.

sat nam
wahe guru